Disclaimer

All erudition contained in this book is given for informational and educational purposes only. The author is not in any way accountable for any results or outcomes that emanate from using this material. Constructive attempts have been made to provide information that is both accurate and effective, but the author is not bound for the accuracy or use/misuse of this information.

The Kybalion

The Forbidden Knowledge of the Hermetic Philosophy and The Universal Laws - Understanding the Art of Hermetic Alchemy and the 7 Principles

By Elijah D. Evans

Hermes Trismegistus, The Three Initiates and William Walker Atkinson

Contents

Introduction

The Kybalion is a profound text that expounds on the principles of Hermetic philosophy, an esoteric and spiritual tradition whose origins can be traced back to ancient Egypt and Greece. According to Hermetic teachings, it was in Egypt that the fundamental occult and esoteric knowledge that has influenced the philosophies of all nations, races and peoples for thousands of years was first taught. The land of Egypt was considered the birthplace of the hidden wisdom and mystic teachings, from which other nations such as India, Persia, Chaldea, China, Japan, ancient Greece and Rome, among others, borrowed liberally from the great store of mystical and occult lore that the masterminds of that ancient land had gathered together.

Egypt was home to great adepts and masters who have never been surpassed nor equaled in the centuries that have passed since the days of the Great Hermes. In fact, the Great Lodge of Lodges of the Mystics was located in ancient Egypt, and it was at the doors of its temples that neophytes entered, later to become hierophants, adepts and masters, traveling to the four corners of the earth, imparting the precious knowledge that they had acquired to those who were ready to receive it.

The Kybalion highlights one particular master of Ancient Egypt, who was hailed as "The Master of Masters," known as Hermes Trismegistus. He was considered the father of occult wisdom, the founder of astrology, and the discoverer of alchemy. However, the details of his life story have been lost to history due to the passage of time, though several ancient countries vied over the honor of providing his birthplace, thousands of years ago. The best authorities consider him to be a contemporary of Abraham, and some Jewish traditions claim that Abraham learned some of his mystic knowledge from Hermes himself.

The teachings of Hermes Trismegistus were revered in all ancient lands, and his name was synonymous with the "Fount of Wisdom." Even today, the term "hermetic" is used to mean "secret," "sealed so that nothing can escape," and so on, because the followers of Hermes always observed the principle of secrecy in their teachings. They did not believe in "casting pearls before swine" but instead held to the principle of "milk for babes; meat for strong men." This principle was familiar to readers of the Christian scriptures, but it had been used by the Egyptians for centuries before the Christian era.

The Hermetic Philosophy has been passed down orally from master to student, from initiate to hierophant, and from lip to ear. When it was ever written down, its meaning was veiled in terms of alchemy and astrology. This was necessary to prevent persecution from theologians during the Middle Ages who fought the Secret Doctrine with fire and sword, stake, gibbet, and cross. Even today, few reliable books on the Hermetic Philosophy can be found, despite countless references to it in many books written on various aspects of occultism. Nonetheless, the Hermetic Philosophy is the only Master Key that can unlock all the doors of the Occult Teachings!

It is worth noting that the ancient occultism of India and Persia degenerated and was largely lost because the teachers became priests and mixed theology with philosophy. The result was that the occultism of India and Persia gradually disappeared amongst the mass of religious superstition, cults, creeds, and "gods." The same happened with Ancient Greece and Rome. The Hermetic Teachings of the Gnostics and Early Christians were also lost at the time of Constantine, whose iron hand smothered philosophy with the blanket of theology. This caused the Christian Church to lose that which was its very essence and spirit, and it groped for several centuries for a new understanding of what it meant to be Christian. This led to various schisms and heresies, as different groups struggled to define the nature of Christ and his relationship to God.

One of the most significant events in the early history of Christianity was the Council of Nicaea, which was held in 325 CE. This council was called by the Roman Emperor Constantine in order to settle a dispute within the Church over the nature of Christ. Some believed that Christ was a divine being who was separate from God, while others believed that he was a co-equal member of the Trinity.

The Council of Nicaea resolved this dispute by declaring that Christ was indeed a divine being who was of the same substance as God. This became known as the doctrine of the Trinity, which holds that God is one in essence, but exists as three distinct persons: the Father, the Son (Jesus Christ), and the Holy Spirit.

Over the centuries, Christianity continued to evolve and develop, as different groups interpreted the teachings of Christ in different ways. Today, there are numerous branches of Christianity, each with their own unique beliefs and practices. These include the Roman Catholic Church, the Eastern Orthodox Church, the Anglican Church, and numerous Protestant denominations.

The Seven Principles of The Kybalion

The Kybalion, posits that there exist seven fundamental principles of truth. According to the authors of this ancient work, an individual who understands these principles with true comprehension holds the coveted Magic Key that can unlock all the secrets of the Temple. These Seven Hermetic Principles, which form the bedrock of the entire Hermetic Philosophy, are as follows: The Principle of Mentalism, the Principle of Correspondence, the Principle of Vibration, the Principle of Polarity, the Principle of Rhythm, the Principle of Cause and Effect, and the Principle of Gender.

As we delve deeper into the study of these seven principles, we will gain a more profound understanding of the universe and the workings of the natural world. Each principle builds upon the previous one, creating a cohesive system that allows us to comprehend the intricate complexities of the universe.

The first principle, the Principle of Mentalism, asserts that the universe is fundamentally mental in nature, meaning that all things are created by the mind. The second principle, the Principle of Correspondence, highlights the idea that there is a correspondence between the various planes of existence, such that what happens on one plane is reflected on another.

The Principle of Vibration, the third principle, states that everything in the universe is in constant motion and vibrates at a specific frequency. The fourth principle, the Principle of Polarity, emphasizes the idea that everything in the universe has its opposite, and that these opposites are complementary and necessary for each other's existence.

The fifth principle, the Principle of Rhythm, explains that everything in the universe moves in a cyclical manner and that there are patterns of rhythm that are present in all things. The sixth principle, the Principle of Cause and Effect, posits that everything that occurs in the universe has a cause and effect, and that nothing happens by chance or coincidence.

Finally, the seventh principle, the Principle of Gender, recognizes that there is a masculine and feminine energy present in all things, and that these energies are necessary for creation and manifestation to occur.

As we embark on the journey to understand these seven principles, we must keep in mind that they are not mere intellectual concepts, but rather a way of life and a path to self-mastery. By studying and embodying these principles, we can unlock the Magic Key that will grant us access to the hidden mysteries of the universe, and ultimately, achieve enlightenment.

The Principle of Mentalism

"The All is Mind; The Universe is Mental."—The Kybalion.

The first of the seven principles of Hermetic Philosophy is the Principle of Mentalism, which embodies the truth that "All is Mind." In other words, the universe is a mental creation of The All, subject to the laws of created things.

The Principle of Mentalism explains that the universe, in all its manifestations, is a projection of the mental world. The All, which is the underlying reality of the universe, is unknowable and undefinable but may be considered a universal, infinite, living mind. The phenomenal world, including matter, energy, and all that we perceive with our material senses, is a creation of the mind of The All. By recognizing the mental nature of the universe, we can easily understand and explain all the varied mental and psychic phenomena that occupy so much of our attention.

Understanding this great Hermetic Principle of Mentalism enables individuals to grasp the laws of the Mental Universe and apply them to their well-being and advancement. By mastering the power of our own minds, we can create and shape our lives and the world around us. This principle emphasizes the importance of the power of thought and the mind in shaping our reality. Without this Master-Key, mastery is impossible, and the student knocks in vain at the many doors of The Temple.

Furthermore, the Principle of Mentalism suggests that there is a fundamental unity between all things in the universe, as they all originate from the same source of creation - the All. By recognizing this unity and understanding the interconnectedness of all things, we can develop a deeper understanding of ourselves and our place in the universe. The old Hermetic Masters wrote, long ages ago: "He who grasps the truth of the Mental Nature of the Universe is well advanced on The Path to Mastery." These words still hold true today.

This principle also sheds light on the true nature of "Energy," "Power," and "Matter" and why and how all of these are subordinate to the mastery of mind. It reveals that everything we perceive as physical matter, energy, or phenomena is actually a manifestation of the mental processes of the universe. By establishing the mental nature of the universe, this principle explains the laws of the Mental Universe and how we can apply them to our advantage.

With the Master-Key of the Principle of Mentalism in their possession, Hermetic students can unlock the many doors of the mental and psychic temple of knowledge and enter them freely and intelligently. This principle is essential for anyone seeking to understand the mysteries of the universe and gain mastery over their own mind and life.

The mental Transmutation

The Principle of Mentalism teaches that everything in the universe is a product of the mind. As such, the power of the mind extends far beyond the limitations of the physical world, and it can be used to transmute not only metals and elements but also mental states, degrees, conditions, poles, and vibrations. This is the essence of the Hermetic art of transmutation, which is a purely mental process that involves changing one mental state into another.

The Hermetists were the original alchemists, astrologers, and psychologists. Hermes, the founder of these schools of thought, taught his followers the secrets of mental transmutation and how to use it to achieve their desired outcomes. Today, modern astronomy, chemistry, and psychology have grown out of the ancient practices of astrology, alchemy, and mystic psychology, respectively.

Despite the modern schools' claims to exclusive ownership of this knowledge, the ancients were not ignorant of the principles of physics, chemistry, and psychology that are the foundation of modern science. The records engraved on the stones of Ancient Egypt show that the ancients had a full comprehensive knowledge of astronomy, with the very building of the Pyramids showing the connection between their design and the study of astronomical science. The fragments of the ancient writings show that they were acquainted with the chemical properties of things. In fact, the ancient theories regarding physics are being slowly verified by the latest discoveries of modern science, notably those relating to the constitution of matter.

The Egyptians were especially skilled in the science of Psychology, particularly in the branches that the modern schools ignore, but which are being uncovered under the name of "psychic science". This is perplexing the psychologists of today, and making them reluctantly admit that "there may be something in it after all."

Beyond the material chemistry, astronomy, and psychology, the ancients possessed a knowledge of transcendental astronomy, called astrology; of transcendental chemistry, called alchemy; of transcendental psychology, called mystic psychology. They possessed the Inner Knowledge as well as the Outer Knowledge, the latter alone being possessed by modern scientists.

Among the many secret branches of knowledge possessed by the Hermetists was that known as Mental Transmutation, which forms the subject matter of this lesson. The word "Transmute" means "to change from one nature, form, or substance, into another; to transform". Accordingly, "Mental Transmutation" means the art of changing and transforming mental states, forms, and conditions, into others. Mental Transmutation is the "Art of Mental Chemistry," a form of practical Mystic Psychology that involves the manipulation of mental energy to achieve desired results.

Through the practice of Mental Transmutation, the Hermetists were able to transform negative thoughts and emotions into positive ones, thereby changing the course of their lives. They understood that the key to success in life was not found in the external world but within oneself, and they used Mental Transmutation as a tool to unlock their inner potential. This knowledge is just as relevant today as it was in ancient times, and anyone who wishes to achieve their goals and fulfill their dreams can benefit from studying this ancient art.

The Principle of Mentalism is a fundamental tenet of the ancient art of Mental Alchemy, which teaches that "The All is Mind." This principle asserts that the universe is essentially mental in nature, and that Mental Transmutation is the art of changing the conditions of the universe in accordance with the three fundamental principles of Matter, Force, and Mind. Mental Transmutation is the "Magic" of which the ancient writers spoke, and although they provided few practical instructions, it is a powerful tool that enables the Master to control both material and mental conditions.

Only the most advanced Mental Alchemists have been able to attain the degree of power necessary to control gross physical conditions such as the elements of Nature, the production or cessation of tempests, earthquakes, and other great physical phenomena. However, the existence of such Masters is a matter of earnest belief to all advanced occultists of all schools. The best teachers assure their students that such Masters exist and have these powers, based on their own experiences. These Masters do not make public exhibitions of their powers, but seek seclusion from the crowds of men to better work toward the Path of Attainment.

The existence of these Masters serves to emphasize the fact that their power is entirely Mental, and operates along the lines of higher Mental Transmutation under the Hermetic Principle of Mentalism, which states that "The Universe is Mental." This principle holds that behind all outward appearances or manifestations, there must always be a Substantial Reality.

When considering the Universe, of which he is a unit, man sees nothing but change in matter, forces, and mental states. He sees that nothing really is, but that everything is becoming and changing. Nothing stands still—everything is being born, growing, dying—the very instant a thing reaches its height, it begins to decline. The law of rhythm is in constant operation—there is no reality, enduring quality, fixity, or substantiality in anything—nothing is permanent but Change.

This law of Change and impermanence is the essence of all existence, and it is through the recognition of this fact that man can come to understand the Substantial Reality that lies behind all things. All thinkers, in all lands and in all times, have assumed the necessity for postulating the existence of this Substantial Reality. All philosophies worthy of the name have been based upon this thought. Men have given to this Substantial Reality many names—some have called it by the term of Deity (under many titles); others have called it "The Infinite and Eternal Energy"; others have tried to call it "Matter"—but all have acknowledged its existence. It is self-evident—it needs no argument.

The concept of Substance and Substantiality is a central tenet of Mental Alchemy, and it refers to the essence, the essential reality, the thing in itself that underlies all outward manifestations. Substance is that which is actually existing, the essential element, and that which is real. Reality, therefore, is the state of being real, true, enduring, valid, fixed, permanent, and actual. The Law of Substance asserts that there is always a Substantial Reality behind every outward appearance, and that this Substantial Reality is the foundation of all existence.

By recognizing the impermanence and changing nature of all things, and by acknowledging the existence of a Substantial Reality that lies behind all outward appearances, the adept Mental Alchemist can unlock the power of Mental Transmutation and become a Master of the Art. It is only through the attainment of this level of knowledge and understanding that one can hope to control both material and mental conditions and achieve true mastery over the forces of the universe.

These Hermetic Masters have led us to identify an Underlying Power, a Substantial Reality, that we refer to as "The All." We consider this term to be the most comprehensive of all those applied by humankind to that which transcends names and labels.

The great Hermetic thinkers of all time, as well as the illuminated souls who have reached higher planes of being, all agree that the inner nature of The All is unknowable. This is a fundamental principle that we accept and teach. The All, being the ultimate power and essence of the universe, can only be comprehended by itself. No mortal mind can even begin to fathom its true nature and being.

The Hermetists maintain that The All, in itself, is and must always remain unknowable. They regard all the theories, guesses, and speculations of theologians and metaphysicians regarding The All's inner nature as nothing but childish efforts of the human mind to grasp the secret of the Infinite. Such endeavors have always failed and will continue to fail, given the very nature of the task at hand.

Anyone who tries to pursue these inquiries will only wander in the labyrinth of thoughts until they lose all reasoning and sanity. They will become unfit for the work of life, just like a squirrel that runs around and around a circling treadmill wheel of its cage, traveling ever but reaching nowhere. In the end, they remain prisoners and stand just where they started.

Even more presumptuous are those who attempt to attribute to The All the personality, qualities, properties, characteristics, and attributes of themselves. They project human emotions, feelings, and characteristics onto The All, such as jealousy, susceptibility to flattery and praise, desire for offerings and worship, and other human-like qualities, which are nothing but survivals from the childhood of our race. These ideas are unworthy of mature men and women and are being rapidly discarded.

In order to understand the nature of The All, it is necessary to distinguish between Religion and Theology, and between Philosophy and Metaphysics. Religion refers to the intuitive realization of the existence of The All and one's relationship to it, while Theology attempts to describe The All in terms of personality, qualities, and characteristics. Philosophy, on the other hand, seeks knowledge of things knowable and thinkable, while Metaphysics aims to go beyond the boundaries of what is knowable and thinkable. Religion and Philosophy are grounded in reality, while Theology and Metaphysics are rooted in ignorance and offer little support for the mind or soul of man.

Although The All is unknowable, there are certain truths about its existence that the human mind must accept. These reports form a suitable subject of inquiry, particularly as they agree with the reports of the Illumined on higher planes. The human reason informs us about The All, and we must accept its reports as long as we think at all.

According to the human reason, The All must be all that really is, and nothing can exist outside of it.

The All must be infinite, with no external definition, confinement, boundary, limit, or restriction. It must be infinite in time, space, and power. It must be eternal and have always continuously existed, for there is nothing else to have created it, and something can never evolve from nothing. It must continuously exist forever, for there is nothing to destroy it, and it can never become nothing.

The All must be immutable, not subject to change in its real nature, and cannot be added to or subtracted from, increased or diminished, or become greater or lesser in any respect whatsoever. It must have always been, and must always remain, just what it is now - The All - and there has never been, is not now, and never will be anything else into which it can change.

Since The All is infinite, absolute, eternal, and unchangeable, anything finite, changeable, fleeting, and conditioned cannot be The All. As there is nothing outside of The All in reality, all finite things must be nothing in reality. Although this may seem contradictory, there is a reconciliation of this idea.

Matter forms the physical foundation for all forms, but The All is not merely Matter. Matter cannot manifest Life or Mind, and as Life and Mind are manifested in the Universe, The All cannot be Matter. Modern Science has abandoned the theory of Matter and now rests on the basis of "Energy," or "interrupted energy or force." However, The All cannot be mere Energy or Force, for if it were, then there would be no such things as Life and Mind in existence. Therefore, The All is neither Matter nor Energy, but something beyond these categories. The nature of The All is ultimately unknowable, and the human mind can only comprehend it to a certain extent.

In short, The All cannot be limited by anything outside of itself, and anything that appears to be outside of itself is merely an illusion created by the limitations of human perception.

It is important to note that while the essential nature of The All is unknowable, there are certain truths connected with its existence that the human mind finds itself compelled to accept. An examination of these reports forms a proper subject of inquiry, particularly as they agree with the reports of the Illumined on higher planes.

The human reason, whose reports we must accept so long as we think at all, informs us as follows regarding The All, and that without attempting to remove the veil of the Unknowable:

(1) The All must be all that really is. There can be nothing existing outside of The All, else The All would not be The All.

(2) The All must be Infinite, for there is nothing else to define, confine, bound, limit, or restrict The All. It must be Infinite in Time, or Eternal—it must have always continuously existed, for there is nothing else to have ever created it, and something can never evolve from nothing, and if it had ever "not been," even for a moment, it would not "be" now—it must continuously exist forever, for there is nothing to destroy it, and it can never "not-be," even for a moment because something can never become nothing. It must be Infinite in Space—it must be Everywhere, for there is no place outside of The All—it cannot be otherwise than continuous in Space, without break, cessation, separation, or interruption, for there is nothing to break, separate, or interrupt its continuity, and nothing with which to "fill in the gaps." It must be Infinite in Power, or Absolute, for there is nothing to limit, restrict, restrain, confine, disturb, or condition it—it is subject to no other Power, for there is no other Power.

(3) The All must be immutable, or not subject to change in its real nature, for there is nothing to work changes upon it; nothing into which it could change, nor from which it could have changed. It cannot be added to nor subtracted from; increased nor diminished; nor become greater or lesser in any respect whatsoever. It must have always been, and must always remain, just what it is now—The All—there has never been, is not now, and never will be, anything else into which it can change.

The All being Infinite, Absolute, Eternal, and Unchangeable, it must follow that anything finite, changeable, fleeting, and conditioned cannot be The All. And as there is Nothing outside of The All, in Reality, then any and all such finite things must be as Nothing in Reality. Now do not become befogged, nor frightened—we are not trying to lead you into the Christian Science field under cover of Hermetic Philosophy. There is a Reconciliation of this apparently contradictory state of affairs. Be patient, we will reach it in time. We see around us that which is called "Matter," which forms the physical foundation for all forms. Is The All merely Matter? Not at all! Matter cannot manifest Life or Mind, and as Life and Mind are manifested in the Universe, The All cannot be Matter, for nothing rises higher than its own source—nothing is ever manifested in an effect that is not in the cause—nothing is evolved as a consequent that is not involved as an antecedent. And then Modern Science informs us that there is really no such thing as Matter—that what we call Matter is merely "interrupted energy or force," that is, energy or force at a low rate of vibration. In other words, everything in the physical universe, including the human body, is made up of energy.

The implications of this understanding are profound. If everything is energy, then we are all connected to everything else in the universe. Our thoughts and emotions, which are also forms of energy, can have a powerful impact on our physical and mental well-being, as well as on the world around us. This is the basis of many holistic and alternative healing practices that focus on the mind-body connection. Moreover, the idea that we are all connected in this way suggests that we are part of a larger, interconnected whole. Many spiritual traditions and belief systems have long held this view, and it is becoming increasingly recognized in scientific circles as well. This sense of connection and unity can be a powerful source of meaning and purpose in our lives. In summary, the idea that everything is energy challenges our traditional notions of the world as made up of separate, discrete objects and invites us to see ourselves and our world in a new light. It can also provide a framework for understanding the mind-body connection and the interdependence of all things.

The Divine Paradox

In the search for understanding, some individuals might believe that they can defy the laws of the universe. However, these people are foolish and vain, as they will inevitably be broken against the rocks and torn asunder by the elements. On the other hand, the truly wise understand the nature of the universe and use its laws against itself. By utilizing the art of alchemy, they transmute what is undesirable into what is worthy, thereby triumphing. True mastery is not found in abnormal dreams, visions, or fantastic imaginings, but rather in using higher forces against the lower. By vibrating on the higher planes, they escape the pains of the lower ones. Transmutation, not presumptuous denial, is the weapon of the master.

This is the paradox of the universe that results from the principle of polarity. It manifests when The All begins to create. It is essential to understand it, for it points to the difference between half-wisdom and wisdom. To The Infinite All, the universe, its laws, powers, life, and phenomena are like things witnessed in the state of meditation or dream. However, to all that is finite, the universe must be treated as real. Life and action must be based on this understanding, though always with an ever-growing understanding of higher truth. Each must act according to its own plane and laws.

Were The All to imagine that the universe were indeed reality, then woe to the universe. There would be no escape from the lower to the higher divineward, and the universe would become a fixity where progress would be impossible. Similarly, if man, owing to half-wisdom, acts and lives and thinks of the universe as merely a dream akin to his own finite dreams, then it becomes so for him. He stumbles around in a circle, making no progress and only awakening at last by falling bruised and bleeding over the natural laws he ignored. It is essential to keep the mind ever on the star, but the eyes must watch over one's footsteps, lest they fall into the mire by reason of their upward gaze.

Remember the divine paradox: while the universe is not, it still is. Remember ever the two poles of truth, the absolute and the relative. Beware of half-truths. Hermetists know as "the Law of Paradox," an aspect of the principle of polarity. The Hermetic writings are filled with references to the appearance of the paradox in the consideration of the problems of life and being. The teachers warn their students against the error of omitting the "other side" of any question, particularly the problems of the absolute and the relative, which perplex all students of philosophy and cause so many to think and act contrary to what is generally known as "common sense."

We caution all students to be sure to grasp the divine paradox of the absolute and relative, lest they become entangled in the mire of the half-truth. This particular lesson has been written with this view in mind. The first thought that comes to the thinking man after realizing the truth that the universe is a mental creation of The All is that the universe and all that it contains is a mere illusion, an unreality. However, this, like all other great truths, must be considered from the absolute and the relative points of view.

From the absolute viewpoint, the universe is in the nature of an illusion, a dream, a phantasmagoria, as compared to The All in itself. This element of impermanence and change, finiteness, and unsubstantiality must ever be connected with the idea of a created universe when contrasted with the idea of The All, no matter what may be our beliefs concerning the nature of both. Philosophers, metaphysicians, scientists, and theologians all

As we delve deeper into the teachings of Hermeticism, it is important to understand that the concept of the universe being unsubstantial is not unique to this philosophy. Many other schools of thought have recognized the impermanence and illusory nature of our world. From the perspective of the Absolute, there is nothing that exists except for The All, and everything else is a mere product of time, space, and change. Whether we conceive of the universe as being composed of matter or as a creation of The All's mental faculties, it is ultimately unreal and non-enduring.

This may seem like a startling revelation, but it is crucial to recognize before passing judgment on Hermeticism's conception of the mental nature of the universe. To truly grasp the nature of reality, we must consider all other conceptions and see that this view holds true for them as well. However, it is important to note that while the Absolute view may hold that the universe is unreal and illusionary, it is still very real to finite minds that are a part of that universe and perceive it through mortal faculties.

It is important to understand that the Absolute Truth, which is defined as "Things as the mind of God knows them," is not the only truth. There is also Relative Truth, which is "Things as the highest reason of Man understands them." While the universe may be unreal from The All's perspective, it is still very real to us. We must recognize the Absolute view without denying the facts and phenomena of the universe as they present themselves to us. We are not The All, and therefore, we must not make the mistake of ignoring or denying our finite existence.

We perceive matter with our senses, and it is real to us, but from a scientific point of view, there is no such thing as matter. Rather, matter is seen as an aggregation of atoms, which are themselves a grouping of units of force called electrons or ions, vibrating and in constant circular motion. The stone that we kick may seem real, but it is ultimately made up of the same units of force that our own body is composed of.

Similarly, the mental images created in the minds of artists, sculptors, authors, and dramatists seem very real to them. We can recognize the characters and emotions they portray and empathize with them. If we, as finite beings, can perceive the reality in the mental images created by other finite beings, imagine the degree of reality in the Mental Images created in the Mind of the Infinite! To us, this universe of Mentality is very real indeed, and it is the only one we can ever know, even as we rise from plane to plane of existence.

It is true that as we rise higher in the scale, the illusory nature of finite things becomes more apparent, but it is only when The All withdraws us into itself that the vision actually vanishes. We need not dwell upon the feature of illusion, but rather recognize the real nature of the universe and seek to understand its mental laws. These laws are no less ironclad because of the mental nature of the universe. All beings, except The All, are bound by them.

What is in the Infinite Mind of The All is real in a degree second only to that Reality itself which is vested in the nature of The All. There is no need to feel insecure or afraid as we are all held firmly in the Infinite Mind of The All. There is no power outside of The All that can affect us. We may rest calm and secure, knowing that we are part of something greater than ourselves. This realization brings us a world of comfort and security that we may draw upon as we travel from plane to plane of being.

As we rest peacefully in the Cradle of the Deep, rocked by the gentle rhythm of the ocean, we are reminded of the infinite power of the Ocean of Infinite Mind - The All. It is within The All that we live and move and have our being. Though we dwell on the plane of Matter, we understand that it is simply an aggregation of rapidly vibrating electrons, or particles of Force, gyrating around each other in the formation of atoms. These atoms vibrate and gyrate, forming molecules, which then form larger masses of Matter. However, Matter remains Matter to us, and we cannot deny its existence in its relative aspect. The Laws of Nature, too, remain constant and effective, and we cannot deny their existence. They are Mental creations of The All, and they are in full effect on the various planes. The most advanced Masters may acquire the powers usually attributed to the gods of men, and there are countless ranks of being whose power transcends even that of the highest Masters among men. Yet, even these highest Beings must bow to the Law and be subservient to it, for nothing but The All can escape Law. Mortal man, therefore, should not consider the Laws of Nature as unreal or illusory, simply because they are Mental in nature.

These Laws which The All intends to be governing Laws are not to be defied or argued away, for they form the framework that holds the Universe together.

The Hermetic Principle of Mentalism does not change the scientific conceptions of the Universe, Life, or Evolution. Rather, it explains the true nature of the Universe on the principle that all is Mental, while modern science has taught that it is Material or Energy at the last analysis. The two teachings, in fact, corroborate each other. It is through the application of higher forces that we can control Matter, and in doing so, we recognize its phenomena. However, we cannot escape Law or rise above it entirely, for even the highest Master and Being must bow to the Law and be as Nothing in the eye of The All. As mortal beings, we should not attempt to ignore the relative aspect of Matter, at least not while we dwell on its plane. Instead, we should seek to understand the Laws of Nature and apply the higher forces to overcome the lower ones. By doing so, we recognize the power of The All and our place within the Universe.

The Hermetic Teachings find no fault with the basic principle of Herbert Spencer, which postulates the existence of an "Infinite and Eternal Energy, from which all things proceed." In fact, the Hermetics recognize in Spencer's philosophy the highest outside statement of the workings of the Natural Laws that have ever been promulgated. They believe that Spencer was a reincarnation of an ancient philosopher who dwelt in ancient Egypt thousands of years ago, and who later incarnated as Heraclitus, the Grecian philosopher who lived b.c. 500. They regard his statement of the "Infinite and Eternal Energy" as directly in the line of the Hermetic Teachings, always with the addition of their own doctrine that his "Energy" is the Energy of the Mind of The All.

The Master-Key of the Hermetic Philosophy allows the student of Spencer to unlock many doors of the inner philosophical conceptions of the great English philosopher, whose work shows the results of the preparation of his previous incarnations.

His teachings regarding Evolution and Rhythm are in almost perfect agreement with the Hermetic Teachings regarding the Principle of Rhythm. Therefore, the student of Hermetics need not lay aside any of his cherished scientific views regarding the Universe. All he is asked to do is to grasp the underlying principle of "The All is Mind; the Universe is Mental—held in the Mind of The All."

The other six of the Seven Principles will "fit into" his scientific knowledge, and will serve to bring out obscure points and to throw light in dark corners. This is not to be wondered at, considering the influence of the Hermetic thought on the early philosophers of Greece, upon whose foundations of thought the theories of modern science largely rest. The acceptance of the First Hermetic Principle (Mentalism) is the only great point of difference between Modern Science and Hermetic students, and Science is gradually moving toward the Hermetic position in its groping in the dark for a way out of the Labyrinth into which it has wandered in its search for Reality.

To impress upon the minds of our students the fact that the Universe and its laws and phenomena are just as real, so far as Man is concerned, as they would be under the hypotheses of Materialism or Energism, is the purpose of this lesson. Under any hypothesis, the Universe in its outer aspect is changing, ever-flowing, and transitory, and therefore devoid of substantiality and reality. But, note the other pole of the truth, under any of the same hypotheses, we are compelled to act and live as if the fleeting things were real and substantial.

Thus, the Hermetic Teachings do not require the student to abandon scientific knowledge, but to expand upon it and view it through the lens of Mentalism. The Hermetics recognize the importance of scientific inquiry, but they also understand that it cannot be the sole means of understanding the Universe. In the end, what matters is not the particular hypothesis we choose to explain the world, but rather how we choose to live and act within it. Whether we see the Universe as material or mental, we must still navigate its complexities and transience with the same care and attention.

The world we live in is not one of dreams, but a universe with natural laws and forces that govern our lives. Mentalism, a belief system that recognizes the power of the mind as the greatest natural force, revolutionizes life for those who understand its principles and laws. Under the old views, mental power was ignored as a natural force, but Mentalism brings it to the forefront. This difference is significant, and it calls upon students to grasp the advantages of Mentalism and learn how to apply its laws in their lives.

However, as The Kybalion cautions, students must not fall prey to the temptation that overcomes the half-wise. They become hypnotized by the apparent unreality of things, wandering about like dream-people and ignoring the practical work and life of man. The result of such folly is that they are broken against the rocks and torn asunder by the elements.

Instead, students must follow the example of the wise, who use the laws to their advantage. They use law against laws, the higher against the lower, and by the art of alchemy, transmute that which is undesirable into that which is worthy. This triumph of the wise shows the way forward for students of Mentalism.

The mastery of Mentalism does not consist of abnormal dreams, visions, and fantastic imaginings or living, but in using the higher forces against the lower, escaping the pains of the lower planes by vibrating on the higher. Transmutation, not presumptuous denial, is the weapon of the Master. These insights from The Kybalion are essential teachings for any student of Mentalism.

It is crucial to remember that our business in the universe is not to deny its existence, but to live using the laws to rise from lower to higher, doing the best that we can under the circumstances arising each day, and living to our highest ideas and ideals. The true meaning of life is not known to men on this plane, but our own intuitions and the highest authorities teach us that we will make no mistake in living up to the best that is in us, realizing the universal tendency in the same direction in spite of apparent evidences to the contrary.

We are all on The Path, and the road leads upward ever, with frequent resting places. The Message of The Kybalion is worth reading and committing to memory for any student of Mentalism. By following the example of the wise and avoiding the mistake of the half-wise who perish by reason of their folly, we can find the way forward on our journey to self-mastery.

“The All” in All

Throughout history, the phrase "All in All" has been used to refer to a person's deity, but little do people know that this phrase holds a hidden truth, an inner occult truth that has been concealed for centuries. This phrase is a remnant of the ancient Hermetic Maxim that holds great importance in philosophy, science, and religion. To understand this truth is to gain great knowledge. The Hermetic Teaching reveals that the Universe is Mental, held within the Mind of The All, and "All is in The All." However, it is also equally true that "The All is in all." This may seem contradictory, but it is reconcilable under the Law of Paradox and an exact Hermetic statement of the relations between The All and its Mental Universe.

Let us now examine the other aspect of the subject. The Hermetic Teachings state that The All is Imminent in its Universe, which means that it remains within, inherent, and abiding within every part, particle, unit, or combination within the Universe. The Principle of Correspondence usually illustrates this statement. The Teacher instructs the student to form a Mental Image of something, such as a person, an idea, or something with a mental form. The student will find that while the image exists solely within their mind, they are immanent in the mental image as well. In other words, the entire virtue, life, and spirit of the mental image are derived from the "immanent mind" of the thinker.

To better understand this concept, let us consider the characters created by Shakespeare or the Venus of Medici, the Sistine Madonna, and the Apollo Belvedere. Did these characters and sculptures have a personal spirit independent of their creator? The Law of Paradox explains that both propositions are true, viewed from the proper viewpoints. The characters and sculptures represent the spiritual and mental power of their creators, but they also have spirits and reality of their own. Micawber is both Micawber and Dickens. While Micawber may be said to be Dickens, Dickens is not identical to Micawber.

The All is in the earth-worm, and yet the earth-worm is far from being The All. And still, the wonder remains, that though the earth-worm exists merely as a lowly thing, created and having its being solely within the Mind of The All, yet The All is immanent in the earth-worm and in the particles that go to make up the earth-worm. Can there be any greater mystery than this of "All in The All, and The All in All?"

The above illustrations are necessarily imperfect and inadequate, for they represent the creation of mental images in finite minds, while the Universe is a creation of Infinite Mind. However, it is merely a matter of degree—the same Principle is in operation—the Principle of Correspondence manifests in each—"As above, so Below; as Below, so above." And, in the degree that Man realizes the existence of the Indwelling Spirit immanent within his being, so will he rise in the spiritual scale of life.

The understanding of the truth behind the phrase "All in All" holds great importance, as it is one of the greatest philosophical, scientific, and religious truths. It is a hidden truth that has been passed down through the ages, and to those who truly understand this truth, great knowledge is gained. The Universe is Mental, and "All is in The All." The All is Immanent in its Universe, and the Principle of Correspondence is at work in every part, particle, unit, or combination within the Universe. This truth is not only a matter of degree but also a matter of understanding, for the more one realizes the existence of the Indwelling Spirit immanent within his being, the more he will be able to tap into the boundless power and wisdom of the Universe. As the Kybalion says, "He who grasps the truth of the Mental Nature of the Universe is well advanced on the path to mastery."

This understanding is not limited to any particular philosophy, religion, or scientific system. It is a universal truth that has been recognized by seekers of truth throughout the ages. Whether one is a student of Hermeticism, Buddhism, Christianity, or any other path, the realization of this truth can lead to a deeper understanding of the nature of reality and the purpose of life.

The idea that "All is in The All, and The All is in All" is both simple and profound. It speaks to the interconnectedness of all things, the oneness of the Universe, and the essential unity of all existence. It reminds us that we are not separate from the Universe but are an integral part of it. It calls us to recognize our own divinity and to awaken to the limitless potential that lies within us.

To truly understand this truth, one must go beyond intellectual knowledge and experience it directly. This requires a shift in consciousness, a letting go of limiting beliefs and a surrendering to the wisdom and power of the Universe. It is a journey of self-discovery and self-realization that leads to greater peace, harmony, and fulfillment.

Spiritual development refers to the recognition, realization, and manifestation of the Spirit within us. This is the essence of True Religion, and it is the truth that all beings on the path to spiritual enlightenment must remember. The universe consists of many planes of being, sub-planes of life, and degrees of existence, and everything depends on the advancement of beings along the scale. The lowest point on the scale is the grossest matter, while the highest point is separated from the Spirit of The All by the thinnest division.

All beings are moving upward and onward along the Scale of Life, and all progress is a Returning Home. Despite all the seemingly contradictory appearances, everything is moving upward and onward. This is the message of the Illumined.

According to Hermetic Teachings, the process of the Mental Creation of the Universe begins with The All, in its aspect of "Being," projecting its Will toward its aspect of "Becoming," thus beginning the process of creation. This process involves the lowering of vibration until the grossest possible form of Matter is manifested, at which point the stage of Involution is reached. The All becomes "involved" or "wrapped up" in its creation, similar to how an artist, writer, or inventor becomes so absorbed in their mental creation that they almost forget their own existence.

This involuntary stage of Creation is sometimes called the "Outpouring" of the Divine Energy, and the Evolutionary state is called the "Indrawing." The furthest pole of the Creative process is considered to be the furthest removed from The All, while the beginning of the Evolutionary stage marks the beginning of the return swing of the pendulum of Rhythm. All Hermetic Teachings hold the "coming home" idea.

During the "Outpouring," the vibrations become lower and lower until the urge ceases, and the return swing begins. However, from the beginning of the Evolutionary or "Indrawing" stage, the Law of Individualization is manifested, meaning there is a tendency to separate into Units of Force. As a result, unindividualized energy that left The All returns as countless highly developed Units of Life, having risen higher and higher in the scale through Physical, Mental, and Spiritual Evolution.

The ancient Hermetists had a specific term, "Meditation," which they used to describe the process of mental creation of the Universe in the mind of The All. They also used the term "Contemplation" frequently. Essentially, the Hermetic Teachings regard the process of Evolution as the result of The All employing its Divine Attention. The word "Attention" is derived from the Latin root meaning "to reach out; to stretch out," indicating that the act of Attention is essentially a mental "reaching out; extension" of mental energy. Therefore, when The All is said to employ its Divine Attention, it is engaging in a mental "reaching out" to create the Universe.

The Hermetic Teachings maintain that The All, having meditated upon the beginning of the Creation, established the material foundations of the Universe, thought it into existence, and then gradually awakened from its Meditation. This awakening sets into motion the process of Evolution on the material, mental, and spiritual planes, successively and in order. Thus, the upward movement begins, and all things begin to move Spiritward. Matter becomes less gross, the Units spring into being, combinations begin to form, Life appears and manifests in higher and higher forms, and Mind becomes more and more evident, with vibrations constantly increasing.

The entire process of Evolution, in all of its phases, begins and proceeds according to the established Laws of the "Indrawing" process. Each æon contains countless millions of years, and the entire process of Creation, including Involution and Evolution of a Universe, is but "as the twinkle of the eye" to The All, even though it takes aeons upon aeons of Man's time to complete. At the end of countless cycles of aeons, The All withdraws its attention from the Universe, having completed the Great Work, and is withdrawn back into The All from which it emerged. However, the Spirit of each soul is not annihilated but infinitely expanded, and the Created and the Creator are merged.

The illustration of The All's meditation and subsequent awakening is an attempt by the Teachers to describe the infinite process using a finite example. It is essential to note that the difference between the macrocosm and the microcosm is only in degree. Just as The All arouses itself from its meditation upon the Universe, humans, in time, cease to manifest upon the Material Plane and withdraw themselves more and more into the Indwelling Spirit, which is, indeed, "The Divine Ego."

There is one more matter of which we desire to speak in this lesson, and that comes very near to an invasion of the Metaphysical field of speculation, although our purpose is merely to show the futility of such speculation. The question of "Why does The All create Universes?" is one that inevitably comes to the mind of all thinkers who seek the Truth. The question may be asked in various forms, but the gist of the inquiry is the same. However, the Hermetic Teachings maintain that such speculation is futile, and it is unnecessary to seek the answer to this question.

The question of why The All, the supreme and infinite power, created and manifested the universe has been pondered by men for ages, yet no answer has ever truly satisfied. Some have suggested that The All had something to gain by creation, but such an idea is absurd, for what could The All possibly gain that it did not already possess?

Others have theorized that The All created out of a desire for love, pleasure, or amusement, or perhaps because it was lonely or wished to display its power. However, these explanations are juvenile and belong to a period of thought long surpassed.

Others have posited that The All was compelled to create due to its internal nature or creative instinct. This idea is more advanced than the previous ones, yet it still falls short in the assertion that The All can be compelled by anything, whether internal or external. If The All were compelled by its internal nature or creative instinct, then that would make it the Absolute instead of The All, rendering the proposition flawed.

Despite these shortcomings, The All still creates and manifests, implying the existence of an infinite desire and will within it, akin to an "inner nature" or "creative instinct" in man. The All could not act unless it desired to do so and would not desire to act unless it derived some satisfaction from it. These actions and desires are part of The All's "inner nature" and may exist according to the Law of Correspondence. However, it is preferable to think of The All as acting independently of any influence, internal or external.

The root of the problem lies in the fact that The All's actions cannot be explained by reason or cause. The All is above cause and effect except when it chooses to become a cause, at which point the principle is set into motion. Thus, The All acts simply because it acts, and it is impossible to speculate on the reason for its actions.

The answer to this question is locked within the inner self of The All, along with its secret of being. The Law of Correspondence only reaches the aspect of The All known as "The Aspect of Becoming," while the "Aspect of Being" lies beyond it. In this aspect, all laws and principles merge into one, and The All, principle, and being are identical, one and the same. Metaphysical speculation on this point is futile, and even the great Hermes refused to provide an answer when asked by his students, pressing his lips together and saying nothing.

It is said that the lips of Wisdom are closed except to the ears of Understanding, and perhaps even advanced students like Hermes' were not worthy of the teaching.

Regardless of whether an answer exists, the truth remains that "While All is in The All, it is equally true that The All is in All." This knowledge is profound, and those who truly understand it have attained great knowledge. Even if the question remains unanswered, the pursuit of understanding The All and its place in the universe is a noble and worthwhile endeavor.

The Principle of Correspondence.

"As above, so below; as below, so above."—The Kybalion.

The principle of correspondence is an ancient and fundamental concept that asserts that there is always a correspondence between the laws and phenomena of the various planes of being and life. This principle is encapsulated in the Hermetic axiom "As above, so below; as below, so above." It is a key to unlocking the secrets of nature and solving many dark paradoxes. By understanding this principle, we gain a means of understanding much that would otherwise be unknowable.

The principle of correspondence is universal and manifests in the various planes of the material, mental, and spiritual universe. The ancient Hermetists considered this principle to be one of the most important mental instruments by which man was able to pry aside the obstacles that hid from view the unknown. Its use even tore aside the veil of Isis, revealing a glimpse of the face of the goddess.

This principle is like a key that unlocks the mysteries of the universe. Just as knowledge of the principles of geometry enables man to measure distant suns and their movements from his observatory, knowledge of the principle of correspondence enables man to reason intelligently from the known to the unknown. By studying the monad, he can understand the archangel.

The Principle of Correspondence is reflected in all things in the universe. For example, the patterns and laws that govern the movement of planets in the solar system are reflected in the movement of electrons around the nucleus of an atom. Similarly, the emotions and thoughts that we experience on a personal level are reflected in the larger collective consciousness of humanity. By understanding the Principle of Correspondence, we can gain a deeper understanding of the interconnectedness of all things in the universe.

Through the use of the Principle of Correspondence, we can learn to navigate and work with these principles to manifest our desires and achieve our goals. This principle is often used in practices such as astrology, divination, and meditation, as it allows us to tap into the larger patterns and energies that govern the universe. By understanding and applying this principle in our lives, we can align ourselves with the universe and become co-creators with the divine.

Therefore, the Principle of Correspondence is not only a tool for understanding the mysteries of the universe but also a practical tool for personal and spiritual growth. As we come to understand this principle and apply it in our lives, we can begin to see the interconnectedness of all things and realize our true potential as human beings.

The plane of correspondence

The universe is a vast and complex system of planes and dimensions, each of which is governed by its own set of laws and principles. But despite the apparent differences between these planes, they are all interconnected and interdependent, forming a vast network of energy and vibration that permeates all of creation. This is the fundamental truth that lies at the heart of the Second Hermetic Principle: the principle of correspondence.

According to this principle, all planes of existence are in perfect harmony and correspondence with one another. They may appear to be separate and distinct from each other, but they are all part of the same unified whole, and everything in the universe is connected by the same underlying principles and characteristics. Whether we are talking about the physical, mental, or spiritual planes, the same laws apply to all.

To help us better understand the nature of these planes, the Hermetic Philosophy divides the universe into three main categories: the Great Physical Plane, the Great Mental Plane, and the Great Spiritual Plane. Each of these planes represents a different level of manifestation and consciousness, with the lowest point being undifferentiated matter and the highest point being that of spirit. However, these divisions are not set in stone, and the different planes blend into each other in ways that are not always easy to define or categorize.

So what exactly is a plane, and how does it relate to the larger concept of dimensionality? This is a question that has puzzled many people over the years, but the answer is actually quite simple: a plane is a degree of dimension on a scale that can be measured. While it is not a place with ordinary dimensions of space, it is also not just a state or condition. Rather, it is a level of vibration and energy that can be measured and quantified, and which serves as the standard for establishing the degrees or "planes."

This Fourth Dimension, known as the "Dimension of Vibration," is the key to understanding the nature of the planes and their interrelationships. It is the force that drives everything in the universe, from the highest spiritual planes to the lowest physical ones, and it is the foundation upon which all of creation is built. By understanding the principles of vibration and energy, we can gain a deeper understanding of the interconnectedness of all things in the universe, and learn to work with these principles to manifest our desires and achieve our goals.

However, the Three Great Planes should not be regarded as actual divisions of the Universe's phenomena, but rather as arbitrary terms used by the Hermetists to aid in the thought and study of the various degrees and forms of universal activity and life. The atom of matter, the unit of force, the mind of man, and the being of the archangel are all degrees in one scale and fundamentally the same. The difference between them is solely a matter of degree and rate of vibration, as all are creations of The All and have their existence solely within the Infinite Mind of The All.

The Hermetists further divide each of the Three Great Planes into Seven Minor Planes, and each of these is also subdivided into seven sub-planes. These divisions are more or less arbitrary, shading into each other, and adopted primarily for the convenience of scientific study and thought.

The Great Physical Plane and its Seven Minor Planes comprise everything related to physics, or material things, forces, and manifestations. It encompasses all forms of matter as well as all forms of energy or force. However, it is important to keep in mind that the Hermetic Philosophy does not recognize Matter as a "thing in itself" or as having a separate existence within The All's Mind. According to the teachings, Matter is simply a form of Energy, Energy with a low rate of vibrations of a specific kind. Consequently, the Hermetists classify Matter as Energy and assign it three of the Seven Minor Planes of the Great Physical Plane.

The Seven Minor Physical Planes are:

I. The Plane of Matter (A)
II. The Plane of Matter (B)
III. The Plane of Matter (C)
IV. The Plane of Ethereal Substance
V. The Plane of Energy (A)
VI. The Plane of Energy (B)
VII. The Plane of Energy (C)

The Plane of Matter (A) includes the forms of matter in their solid, liquid, and gaseous states, as generally recognized by physics textbooks.

The Plane of Matter (B) comprises higher and more subtle forms of matter that modern science is only now beginning to recognize. The phenomena of Radiant Matter, such as radium, belong to the lower subdivision of this minor plane.

The Plane of Matter (C) is composed of forms of the most subtle and tenuous matter, the existence of which is not suspected by ordinary scientists.

The Plane of Ethereal Substance comprises what science speaks of as "The Ether," a substance of extreme tenuity and elasticity that pervades all Universal Space. It acts as a medium for the transmission of waves of energy, such as light, heat, electricity, etc. This Ethereal Substance forms a connecting link between Matter (so-called) and Energy and partakes of the nature of each. The Hermetic Teachings instruct that this plane has seven subdivisions (as do all of the Minor Planes), and that in fact there are seven ethers, instead of just one.

Above the Plane of Ethereal Substance is the Plane of Energy (A), which encompasses the ordinary forms of energy known to science. Its seven sub-planes are heat, light, magnetism, electricity, attraction (including gravitation, cohesion, chemical affinity, etc.), and several other forms of energy indicated by scientific experiments but not yet named or classified.

The Plane of Energy (B) consists of seven sub-planes of higher forms of energy not yet discovered by science. These have been called "Nature's Finer Forces" and are called upon in certain manifestations of mental phenomena, making those phenomena possible.

The Plane of Energy (C) comprises seven sub-planes of highly organized energy that possesses many characteristics of "life." However, it is not recognized by the minds of ordinary men on the plane of development, as it is available for use by beings of the Spiritual Plane alone. The Hermetists describe this energy as "Prana," the universal life-force that animates all living things. This life-force can be directed and utilized by those who have the knowledge and ability to do so.

The beings that employ this energy are seen as "gods" compared even to the highest human types known to us. They are able to perform seemingly miraculous feats, such as healing the sick, controlling the elements, and even raising the dead. The Hermetic Teachings state that these beings are not truly gods but rather advanced beings on the Spiritual Plane who have developed the ability to utilize the energy of Prana in ways that are unimaginable to ordinary humans.

It is said that through diligent study and practice, it is possible for human beings to attain a level of development where they can also harness the power of Prana. However, this requires great discipline and dedication, as well as a deep understanding of the principles and laws of the Universe. The Hermetists emphasize that the path to such mastery is long and arduous, but ultimately rewarding for those who are willing to undertake it.

The Great Mental Plane is an expansive category that encompasses all "living things" familiar to us, as well as others that only occultists recognize. Although the classification of the Seven Minor Mental Planes is somewhat arbitrary, it is still necessary to mention them in order to grasp the full scope of this Plane.

These Seven Minor Mental Planes are as follows:

I. The Plane of Mineral Mind.
II. The Plane of Elemental Mind (A).
III. The Plane of Plant Mind.
IV. The Plane of Elemental Mind (B).
V. The Plane of Animal Mind.
VI. The Plane of Elemental Mind (C).
VII. The Plane of Human Mind.

The Plane of Mineral Mind refers to the states or conditions of entities, groups, and combinations that animate the forms of minerals and chemicals. These entities, referred to as "souls," should not be confused with molecules, atoms, and corpuscles, which are merely the material bodies or forms of these entities. Although the average person does not attribute mind, soul, or life to the Mineral kingdom, occultists recognize their existence, and modern science is moving towards this viewpoint as well.

In fact, molecules, atoms, and corpuscles have their own likes, dislikes, attractions, repulsions, affinities, and non-affinities. Some modern scientific minds believe that the emotions, feelings, desires, and will of atoms differ only in degree from those of humans. The Plane of Mineral Mind is divided into seven sub-divisions, each possessing their own unique characteristics.

The Plane of Elemental Mind (A) comprises the state or condition and degree of mental and vital development of a class of entities unknown to the average person but recognized by occultists. These entities are invisible to the ordinary senses of humans, but they exist and play a part in the Universe. Their degree of intelligence is between that of mineral and chemical entities, and entities of the plant kingdom. The Plane of Elemental Mind (A) also consists of seven sub-divisions, each with their own distinct characteristics.

The Plane of Plant Mind comprises the states or conditions of the entities comprising the kingdoms of the Plant World. Plants, like animals, humans, and super-humans, have life, mind, and souls. This Plane is divided into seven sub-divisions, with each sub-division possessing its own unique qualities.

The Plane of Elemental Mind (B) comprises the states and conditions of a higher form of "elemental" or unseen entities, which play a part in the Universe. The mind and life of these entities form a part of the scale between the Plane of Plant Mind and the Plane of Animal Mind, as they partake of the nature of both. There are also seven sub-divisions to this Plane, each with its own distinct characteristics.

The Plane of Animal Mind comprises the states and conditions of the entities, beings, or souls animating animal forms of life. This kingdom or plane of life is familiar to us all, as we are surrounded by animals in our everyday lives.

The Plane of Elemental Mind (C) comprises entities or beings that are invisible, as all elemental forms are, and that exhibit a nature that combines both animal and human life in varying degrees and combinations. This Plane is divided into seven sub-divisions, with the highest forms being semi-human in intelligence.

The final Plane, the Plane of Human Mind, is divided into seven sub-divisions and comprises manifestations of life and mentality that are common to Man in various grades, degrees, and divisions. It's worth noting that the average modern man only occupies the fourth sub-division of the Plane of Human Mind, with only the most intelligent having crossed the borders into the fifth sub-division. It has taken the race millions of years to reach this stage, and it will take many more years for the race to move on to the sixth and seventh sub-divisions, and beyond.

However, it is important to remember that there have been races before us that have passed through these degrees and on to higher planes. Our own race is the fifth, with stragglers from the fourth, to set foot upon The Path. Moreover, a few advanced souls of our race have outstripped the masses, passed on to the sixth and seventh sub-divisions, and some even further.

The man of the Sixth Sub-Division will be "The Super-Man", and he of the Seventh will be "The Over-Man". These beings will possess superhuman powers and abilities that will seem godlike to those who are not so advanced. They will have unlocked the secrets of the Universe and be able to move through the various planes of existence at will. They will have transcended the limitations of space and time and will be able to manifest their will in the physical world in ways that are inconceivable to us now.

It is important to note that these advanced beings will not be gods in the traditional sense, but rather highly evolved entities who have surpassed the limitations of the human form. They will not be worshiped, but rather respected and revered for their knowledge and wisdom.

It is also worth noting that the development of these advanced beings is not a matter of chance or luck, but rather the result of countless lifetimes of work and effort. Every individual has the potential to evolve to these higher states of consciousness, but it requires dedication, hard work, and a willingness to let go of old habits and beliefs that no longer serve us.

In our previous discussion of the Seven Minor Mental Planes, we only briefly touched upon the Three Elementary Planes. While we won't delve into the topic at length in this work, we feel it's important to offer some clarification on how these planes relate to the more commonly known ones. Think of the Elementary Planes as the black keys on a piano in relation to the white keys. While the white keys alone can produce music, the black keys are necessary for certain scales, melodies, and harmonies. They serve as "connecting links" between different planes, allowing for various forms of development to occur.

This understanding sheds new light on the processes of Evolution, providing a key to the secret door of the "leaps of life" between kingdoms.

Moving on to the Great Spiritual Plane, we encounter beings that are often referred to as Angels, Archangels, and Demi-Gods. These entities are beyond human comprehension, possessing intelligence, power, and being that are akin to what we attribute to Deity. These "Divine" beings are the Elder Brethren of the Race, advanced souls who have progressed beyond the ecstasy of Absorption by The All in order to aid humanity on its journey along The Path. Their existence, along with that of the Angelic Host, plays a crucial role in the Universe's affairs, frequently intervening and offering assistance under the Law of The All.

However, we must remember that even the most advanced of these beings are mortal and subject to the Cosmic Processes and Universal Laws. They exist only as creations of, and in, the Mind of The All. We may use the term "gods" to refer to them, but it's important to understand that they belong to the Universe and are subject to its conditions. Their plane is below that of Absolute Spirit.

Descending to the lower Minor Planes, we encounter great souls known as Masters and Adepts. Above them, incomprehensible Great Hierarchies of the Angelic Hosts reside. These beings, along with the Elder Brethren, exert a powerful influence on Evolution and Cosmic Progress. The occasional intervention of these Unseen Divinities and Angelic Helpers in human affairs has given rise to many legends, beliefs, religions, and traditions throughout history.

The Hermetic Philosophy is a complex and esoteric system that delves into the nature of existence and the powers that manifest on the spiritual planes. Only those who have carefully trained their minds along the lines of this philosophy for years, and those who have brought with them knowledge from previous incarnations, can truly understand the inner teachings regarding these spiritual planes.

The phenomena of the spiritual planes are so much higher than those of the mental planes that attempting to describe them in detail would only result in confusion. Therefore, much of these inner teachings are held by Hermetists as being too sacred, important, and even dangerous for general public dissemination. It is only the most advanced Hermetists who can grasp these teachings, and even then, the knowledge is reserved for a select few.

To occultists, the word "spirit" carries with it the idea of power, living energy, and mystic force. Spiritual power can be employed for both good and evil ends, according to the principle of polarity. This fact has been recognized by most religions, which have their own conceptions of Satan, Beelzebub, the Devil, Lucifer, and Fallen Angels. The knowledge regarding these planes has been kept in the Holy of Holies in all Esoteric Fraternities and Occult Orders, in the Secret Chamber of the Temple.

The consequences of misusing spiritual power are severe, as those who have attained high spiritual powers and have misused them have a terrible fate in store for them. The swing of the pendulum of Rhythm will inevitably swing them back to the furthest extreme of material existence, from which point they must retrace their steps Spiritward along the weary rounds of the Path. However, they always have the added torture of having a lingering memory of the heights from which they fell due to their evil actions. The legends of the Fallen Angels have a basis in actual facts, as all advanced occultists know.

Striving for selfish power on the Spiritual Planes inevitably results in the selfish soul losing its spiritual balance and falling back as far as it had previously risen. But even such a soul is given the opportunity of a return, and such souls make the return journey, paying the terrible penalty according to the invariable Law.

The Hermetic Principles, which apply to all planes of existence, are crucial for understanding the workings of the universe. The Principle of Mental Substance states that all planes are held in the Mind of The All.

The Principle of Correspondence asserts that there is a correspondence, harmony, and agreement between the various planes. The Principle of Vibration explains that the differences between the planes arise from Vibration. The Principle of Polarity is present on each plane, with the extremes of the Poles appearing opposite and contradictory. The Principle of Rhythm describes the ebb and flow, rise and fall, and incoming and outgoing of phenomena. The Principle of Cause and Effect explains that every Effect has its Cause, and every Cause has its effect. Finally, the Principle of Gender manifests on each plane, with Creative Energy being always present and operating along the lines of its Masculine and Feminine Aspects.

The centuries-old Hermetic axiom, "As Above so Below; as Below, so Above," embodies one of the great Principles of Universal Phenomena. This principle speaks to the interconnectedness of all things and the universal nature of the Hermetic Philosophy. As we continue to consider the remaining Principles, we will see even more clearly the truth of the universal nature of this great Principle of Correspondence. The Hermetic Philosophy is a vast and complex system, but with a careful study, one can gain a greater understanding of the workings of the universe and their place within it.

The Principle of Vibration

"Nothing rests; everything moves; everything vibrates."—The Kybalion.

The ancient Hermetic principle of vibration teaches that everything in the universe is in constant motion and vibration, from the tiniest particles to the grandest galaxies. This principle has been echoed in modern science and its latest discoveries, proving the wisdom of the ancient Masters of Ancient Egypt. The fundamental premise of the principle is that varying degrees of vibration account for the differences in matter, energy, mind, and spirit.

At the highest level, the All, which is pure spirit, vibrates at such an immense frequency that it appears to be at rest, just like a rapidly moving wheel that appears motionless. On the other end of the spectrum, the grossest forms of matter appear to be at rest because of their low vibrations. Between these two extremes, there are infinite degrees of vibration, from the smallest particles to the vast expanse of the universe.

This principle extends beyond physical matter to encompass energy and force, mental states, and even spiritual planes. Understanding the vibrational nature of the universe allows us to control our own mental vibrations and those of others. The Masters of Hermeticism apply this principle to the conquering of natural phenomena in various ways, utilizing formulas to harness the power of vibration.

Furthermore, by understanding the Principle of Vibration, we can gain deeper insights into ourselves and the world around us. We possess the power to influence our own vibrations through our thoughts and emotions, which, in turn, can impact the vibrations of the world. Various spiritual practices and healing modalities, such as sound healing, crystal healing, and meditation, utilize the concept of vibrational energy. By working with this principle, we can learn to raise our own vibrational frequency, promoting healing, well-being, and manifesting our desires in the physical world.

Vibration

Throughout the ages, Hermetic teachings have expounded upon the idea that everything in existence is in a state of constant movement and vibration. The differences between the various manifestations of universal power are believed to be solely due to the varying rate and mode of vibrations. Even The All, the essence of universal energy, is said to have a constant vibration of such infinite intensity and rapid motion that it appears to be at rest. The teachers of this ancient philosophy point out that even on the physical plane, a rapidly moving object, such as a revolving wheel, seems to be at rest.

According to the Hermetic Principle of Vibration, Spirit is located at one end of the Pole of Vibration, while the other Pole is comprised of certain extremely gross forms of Matter. Between these two poles, there exist millions upon millions of different rates and modes of vibration. Modern science has confirmed the Hermetic principle that all that we call Matter and Energy are but modes of vibratory motion. Moreover, some of the more advanced scientists are rapidly moving towards the positions of the occultists who hold that the phenomena of Mind are likewise modes of vibration or motion.

All forms of Matter manifest Vibration, and even the particles of Matter are in constant movement and vibration around and against each other. The molecules, which are composed of Atoms, are likewise in constant movement and vibration. These Atoms are composed of Corpuscles, such as "electrons" and "ions," which are in a state of rapid motion, revolving around each other and manifesting a very rapid state and mode of vibration.

Various forms of energy, such as Light, Heat, Magnetism, and Electricity, are said to be forms of vibratory motion that are connected in some way with the Ether, which is believed to be the source of these phenomena.

The Hermeticists postulate the existence of the Universal Ether, which is held to be a higher manifestation of what is erroneously called matter. They refer to it as "The Ethereal Substance."

The Hermeticists believe that this Ethereal Substance is extremely tenuous and elastic, and it pervades universal space, serving as a medium of transmission for waves of vibratory energy, including heat, light, electricity, and magnetism. The Ethereal Substance is a connecting link between the forms of vibratory energy known as "Matter" on the one hand, and "Energy or Force" on the other. It also manifests a degree of vibration, in rate and mode, entirely its own.

Although science does not yet explain the nature of Cohesion, Chemical Affinity, or Gravitation, the Hermeticists have taught for ages past that these three forms of Energy are manifestations of some form of vibratory energy. The Universal Ether, or The Ethereal Substance, serves as a connecting link between the various forms of vibratory energy known to us. It is, therefore, a vital component in understanding the nature of the universe and our place in it.

In order to help readers understand the effects of increasing rates of vibration, scientists often use the illustration of a rapidly moving wheel, top, or cylinder. The illustration begins with an object moving slowly, which can be seen but not heard. However, as the speed of the object increases, a deep growl or low note may be heard, indicating that the rate of vibration has increased. As the rate of vibration continues to increase, the note rises one in the musical scale, and then the next highest note is distinguished.

One after another, all the notes of the musical scale appear, rising higher as the motion increases. Finally, when the vibrations reach a certain rate, the final note perceptible to human ears is reached, and the shrill, piercing shriek dies away into silence. At this point, the human ear cannot register the vibrations of the revolving object anymore, and it becomes completely silent. However, the perception of rising degrees of heat follows, and after quite some time, the object begins to emit a dull, dark reddish color.

As the rate of vibration increases further, the red becomes brighter and eventually melts into an orange, then into a yellow, and finally into the shades of green, blue, indigo, and violet. The violet shades away and all color disappears, as the human eye cannot register them. Nevertheless, there are invisible rays emanating from the revolving object, such as those used in photography and other subtle rays of light.

These peculiar rays are known as the "X Rays," and they begin to manifest as the constitution of the object changes. Moreover, when the appropriate rate of vibration is attained, electricity and magnetism are emitted. As the vibrations of the object increase further, its molecules disintegrate and resolve themselves into the original elements or atoms, which are then separated into the countless corpuscles of which they are composed, following the Principle of Vibration.

Eventually, even the corpuscles disappear, and the object may be said to be composed of the Ethereal Substance. Science does not dare to follow the illustration further, but the Hermetists teach that if the vibrations are continually increased, the object would mount up the successive states of manifestation and would, in turn, manifest the various mental stages, and then, on Spiritward, until it would finally re-enter The All, which is Absolute Spirit. However, the object would have ceased to be an "object" long before the stage of Ethereal Substance was reached. Nevertheless, the illustration is correct inasmuch as it shows the effect of constantly increased rates and modes of vibration.

It is fascinating to think about the potential consequences of increasing rates of vibration, especially when considering the idea that the object may eventually re-enter The All, which is Absolute Spirit. However, such a scenario remains purely theoretical and is beyond the scope of current scientific understanding. Nonetheless, the illustration remains a useful tool for understanding the effects of increasing rates and modes of vibration.

We explored how the Principle of Vibration is evident in the transmission of energy from matter in the form of light and heat. However, the Hermetic Teachings delve deeper into this principle, revealing its power over mental states and conditions.

According to these teachings, all mental states or conditions are accompanied by vibrations that are capable of affecting the minds of others through a process called "induction." This phenomenon, which is becoming increasingly recognized by the public, is the basis of telepathy, mental influence, and other forms of mind-to-mind action and power.

Each thought, emotion, or mental state corresponds to a specific rate and mode of vibration, which can be reproduced through an act of will. By understanding the Principle of Vibration as it applies to Mental Phenomena, one can gain perfect control over their mental states and moods, as well as the ability to influence others' mental states.

In essence, the Hermetic Teachings assert that one can create on the Mental Plane what science creates on the Physical Plane: Vibrations at Will. This power, however, can only be achieved through proper instruction, exercises, and practice in the science of Mental Transmutation, which is one of the branches of the Hermetic Art.

It is clear that the Principle of Vibration has immense power, as evidenced by the abilities of Masters and Adepts who can seemingly disregard the Laws of Nature. They achieve their goals by using one law against another, one principle against another, and by changing the vibrations of material objects or forms of energy. These outcomes are often referred to as "miracles."

As one of the ancient Hermetic writers put it, "He who understands the Principle of Vibration, has grasped the sceptre of Power." The understanding and application of this principle is key to unlocking one's true potential and achieving profound and transformative results in their life and the lives of others.

The Principle of Polarity

"Everything is Dual; everything has poles; everything has its pair of opposites; like and unlike are the same; opposites are identical in nature, but different in degree; extremes meet; all truths are but half-truths; all paradoxes may be reconciled."—The Kybalion.

The Principle of Polarity is a fundamental concept in Hermetic philosophy that embodies the truth that everything in the universe is dual. This principle states that everything has two poles, and that every aspect of the universe has its pair of opposites. The paradoxical nature of this principle has perplexed many, with statements such as "thesis and antithesis are identical in nature but different in degree" and "extremes meet." However, understanding the Principle of Polarity can provide a profound insight into the interconnectedness of the universe.

The principle of polarity operates on both the physical and mental planes, with examples such as heat and cold, light and darkness, and love and hate. While these may appear to be fundamentally different, they are actually different degrees of the same thing. For instance, heat and cold are simply varying degrees of the same thing, with no such thing as absolute heat or absolute cold. The same can be said of light and darkness - they are simply different degrees of electromagnetic radiation.

On the mental plane, the same principle applies to emotions such as love and hate. These are two seemingly opposite mental states, but there are degrees of hate and love, and a middle point where we use terms such as "like" or "dislike." All of these mental states are simply degrees of the same thing, and it is possible to change the vibrations of hate to love using Hermetic formulas.

The Principle of Polarity is not only about understanding the interconnectedness of the universe, but also about achieving greater harmony and balance in our lives.

By embracing both the light and the dark, the positive and the negative, we can achieve a greater understanding of ourselves and the world around us. The Principle of Polarity suggests that in order to understand and appreciate one aspect, we must also understand and appreciate its opposite. By balancing these opposites within ourselves, we can achieve greater harmony and balance in our lives.

The art of polarization becomes a phase of "Mental Alchemy" known and practiced by ancient and modern Hermetic Masters. An understanding of the principle will enable one to change his own polarity, as well as that of others, by devoting the time and study necessary to master the art. The principle of polarity reminds us that everything in the universe is interconnected, and that balance and harmony can only be achieved by recognizing and honoring the polar opposites that exist within and around us.

Polarity

In the pursuit of understanding the underlying principles of the universe, one concept that cannot be ignored is the principle of polarity. According to the teachers who have dedicated their lives to this philosophy, the principle of polarity is omnipresent, and can be found in everything around us. It is a fundamental concept that can be applied across all planes of existence, from the physical to the mental.

To begin with, the teachers explain that Spirit and Matter are the two poles of the same thing, with the intermediate planes being different degrees of vibration. They then proceed to demonstrate that The All and The Many are the same, with the only difference being a matter of degree of Mental Manifestation. This is followed by the assertion that the Law and Laws are the two opposite poles of one thing, as are Principle and Principles, Infinite Mind and finite minds.

Moving on to the Physical Plane, the teachers illustrate the principle by showing that Heat and Cold are identical in nature, with differences only in degree. They use the example of the thermometer, which shows many degrees of temperature, with the lowest pole called "cold" and the highest called "heat." However, there are many degrees of "heat" or "cold" between these poles, and either term is correct. The higher of two degrees is always "warmer," while the lower is always "colder." There is no absolute standard, as all is a matter of degree. There is no place on the thermometer where heat ceases and cold begins; it is all a matter of higher or lower vibrations. Even the terms "high" and "low" are relative, as they are poles of the same thing.

The principle of polarity also applies to other pairs of opposites, such as "East and West," Light and Darkness, the musical scale, and the color scale. Large and Small, Noise and Quiet, Hard and Soft, and Sharp and Dull all follow this rule. Positive and Negative are two poles of the same thing, with countless degrees between them.

Good and Bad are not absolute, as one end of the scale is called Good and the other Bad or Evil, depending on the context. A thing is "less good" than the thing higher in the scale, but that "less good" thing is "more good" than the thing below it, and so on, with "more or less" being regulated by the position on the scale.

This principle also applies to the Mental Plane. "Love and Hate" are generally considered to be diametrically opposed and irreconcilable, but by applying the Principle of Polarity, we find that there is no such thing as Absolute Love or Absolute Hate. The two are simply terms for opposing poles of the same thing. Regardless of where we start on the scale, we find "more love" or "less hate" as we ascend, and "more hate" or "less love" as we descend. There are degrees of Love and Hate, and there is a point in the middle where "Like and Dislike" become so faint that they are difficult to distinguish. This rule also applies to courage and fear.

It is clear that pairs of opposites exist everywhere, and wherever we find one thing, we will also find its polar opposite - the two poles. The teachers believe that this principle is crucial to understanding the workings of the universe, and that by recognizing and accepting it, we can gain a deeper understanding of the world around us. They believe that this principle is essential for anyone who seeks to understand the underlying structure of the universe, and they urge us to contemplate its implications in our daily lives.

The Hermetist's ability to transmute one mental state into another along the lines of polarization is based on the fact that things of the same class can have their polarity changed. This means that Love can become Hate and vice versa, while Courage can become Fear and vice versa, and Hard things can become Soft, and so on. However, things from different classes cannot be transmuted into each other.

The process of transmutation always occurs between objects of the same kind but of varying degrees. For example, a Fearful man can become Courageous by raising his mental vibrations along the Fear-Courage line, and a Slothful man can transform himself into an Active, Energetic individual simply by polarizing along the desired quality line.

The principles of Mental Science can bring about changes in the mental states of individuals, but the underlying principle may not always be clear to the student. Once the Principle of Polarity is understood, and it is recognized that mental changes are caused by a change of polarity, an alteration in degree rather than a transformation into something entirely different, the matter becomes clearer.

To clarify the concept, an analogy from the Physical Plane is used, where it is impossible to change Heat into Sharpness, Loudness, or Highness, but Heat can be transformed into Cold by lowering vibrations. Similarly, Hate and Love, as well as Fear and Courage, are mutually transmutable, but Fear cannot be transformed into Love, and Courage cannot be transmuted into Hate.

There are numerous classes of mental states, each with its own opposing poles along which transmutation is possible. These poles are categorized as Positive and Negative, respectively. Thus, Love is positive to Hate, Courage is positive to Fear, and Activity is positive to Non-Activity, among other things. Even those who are unfamiliar with the Principle of Vibration recognize that the Positive pole appears to be stronger than the Negative and easily dominates it. Nature's tendency is to favor the dominant activity of the Positive pole.

The art of Polarization not only changes one's own mental states but also allows for Mental Influence, where one mind can influence another. Mental Induction is another technique that allows for the production of mental states through "induction" from others.

By bringing one's own mind up to the desired vibration and obtaining the desired polarization, a mental scientist can produce a similar mental state in another person by induction. The result is that the person's vibrations are raised, and they polarize toward the Positive end of the scale instead of the Negative.

The understanding of the Hermetic Principle of Polarity allows the student to better understand their own and others' mental states. These states are all a matter of degree, and understanding this allows one to change their mental poles at will and be the Master of their mental states rather than their servant or slave. By intelligently assisting others and, when desired, changing their polarity, individuals can take control of their mental states and transform themselves into the best version of themselves.

It is recommended that all students become acquainted with the Polarity Principle, as a correct understanding of it will shed light on many difficult subjects. The mastery of this principle is the key to unlocking one's potential and creating positive change in one's life and the lives of others.

The Principle of Rhythm

"Everything flows, out and in; everything has its tides; all things rise and fall; the pendulum-swing manifests in everything; the measure of the swing to the right is the measure of the swing to the left; rhythm compensates."—The Kybalion.

In the world of Hermetics, there is a principle that governs the motion and flow of everything in existence. This principle is known as the Principle of Rhythm. It describes how all things move in a measured and cyclical manner, like a pendulum swinging back and forth, a tide-like ebb and flow, or a rise and fall. This rhythm can be observed in the movements of the sun and the stars, in the cycles of nature, and in the rise and fall of civilizations.

The Principle of Rhythm is closely linked to the Principle of Polarity, which describes how everything in existence has two opposite poles or aspects. These polarities are necessary for balance and harmony, and they are what create the rhythmic motion of the universe.

The Hermetists, who have studied these principles closely, understand that the Principle of Rhythm is an essential part of mental alchemy. By mastering the rhythm of their thoughts and emotions, they are able to achieve a degree of mental poise and firmness that is almost impossible for the masses to comprehend.

The pendulum-swing, which is mentioned in The Kybalion, refers to the movement of energy and consciousness between polar opposites. This swing between positive and negative, joy and sadness, and other polarities is necessary for balance and harmony, and it allows us to appreciate and understand the full range of experiences in life.

The Hermetists have discovered certain means to overcome the effects of the Principle of Rhythm by using appropriate formulas and methods. They apply the Mental Law of Neutralization, which allows them to escape the effects of the pendulum-swing to a certain degree.

By polarizing themselves at the point where they desire to rest and neutralizing the rhythmic swing of the pendulum, they can achieve a greater degree of self-mastery.

By understanding the Principle of Rhythm and embracing the natural ebb and flow of energy and consciousness, we can learn to flow with the rhythms of life, rather than fighting against them. This allows us to achieve greater harmony and balance in our lives, and to navigate the cycles and rhythms of existence with greater ease and understanding.

Rhythms

In the universe, everything is in motion, and this motion is governed by the great Fifth Hermetic Principle, the Principle of Rhythm. This principle asserts that all things exhibit a measured motion that is characterized by a to-and-fro movement, a flow and inflow, a swing forward and backward, a pendulum-like movement, a tide-like ebb and flow, and a high-tide and a low-tide, between the two poles that are manifest on the physical, mental, or spiritual planes.

The Principle of Rhythm is closely related to the Principle of Polarity, which was explained in the preceding chapter. Rhythm manifests between the two poles established by the Principle of Polarity. However, this does not imply that the pendulum of Rhythm swings to the extreme poles, as this rarely occurs. In reality, it swings "towards" one pole and then the other. In all the airs and phenomena of the Universe, there is always action and reaction, advance and retreat, rising and sinking.

This principle is manifested in everything from suns and worlds to men, animals, plants, minerals, forces, energy, mind and matter, and even Spirit. The Principle manifests itself in the creation and destruction of worlds, the rise and fall of nations, the life histories of all things, and finally in Man's mental states.

Beginning with the manifestations of Spirit, of The All, it will be noticed that there is always the Outpouring and the Indrawing, the "Outbreathing and Inbreathing of Brahm", as the Brahmins word it. Universes are created, reach their extreme low point of materiality, and then begin their upward swing. Suns spring into being, and then, having reached their height of power, the process of retrogression begins, and after aeons they become dead masses of matter, awaiting another impulse which starts their inner energies into activity and begins a new solar life cycle.

And thus it is with all the worlds; they are born, grow, and die, only to be reborn. And thus it is with all the things of shape and form; they swing from action to reaction, from birth to death, from activity to inactivity, and then back again. This principle is observable in all living things; they are born, grow, and die, and then they are reborn. So it is with all great movements, philosophies, creeds, fashions, governments, nations, and all else: birth, growth, maturity, decadence, death, and then new birth. The swing of the pendulum is ever in evidence.

The Principle of Rhythm applies to all aspects of human activity. It is applicable everywhere and can be applied to any question or phenomenon on any of life's many planes. The Rhythmic swing from one pole to the other is always available, and the Universal Pendulum is constantly in motion. According to Law, the Tides of Life flow in and out.

In summary, the Principle of Rhythm teaches us that everything in the universe is in motion, and this motion is characterized by a rhythmic swing from one pole to the other. This principle applies to everything from the creation and destruction of worlds to the rise and fall of nations and the life histories of all things. It is a universal principle that can be applied to any question or phenomenon on any of life's many planes.

Modern science has long recognized the Principle of Rhythm as a universal law when it comes to material things. However, the Hermetists have taken this principle to the next level by recognizing its influence on human mental activities. They understood that the Principle of Rhythm is responsible for the perplexing changes in moods and feelings that we experience. But the Hermetic Masters also discovered a way to avoid some of its effects through transmutation.

The Hermetists realized that while the Principle of Rhythm was invariable and ever-present in mental phenomena, there were two planes of its manifestation. They discovered that there were two general planes of consciousness: the Lower and the Higher. This understanding enabled them to rise to the higher plane and thus escape the swing of the Rhythmic pendulum that manifested on the lower plane.

The swing of the pendulum occurred on the Unconscious Plane, and the Consciousness was not affected. They called this the Law of Neutralization.

The Law of Neutralization consists of raising the Ego above the vibrations of the Unconscious Plane of mental activity, so that the negative-swing of the pendulum is not manifested in consciousness, and therefore, they are not affected. It is akin to rising above a thing and letting it pass beneath you. The Hermetic Master or advanced student polarizes themselves at the desired pole and by a process akin to "refusing" to participate in the backward swing, or a "denial" of its influence over them, they stand firm in their polarized position and allow the mental pendulum to swing back along the unconscious plane. All individuals who have attained any degree of self-mastery accomplish this, more or less unknowingly, by refusing to allow their moods and negative mental states to affect them. However, the Master carries this to a much higher degree of proficiency, and by the use of their Will, they attain a degree of Poise and Mental Firmness almost impossible for those who allow themselves to be swung backward and forward by the mental pendulum of moods and feelings.

The importance of the Law of Neutralization becomes apparent when we consider how most people are creatures of moods, feelings, and emotions, and how little mastery of themselves they manifest. The swings of Rhythm have affected everyone at some point in their life. Periods of Enthusiasm are invariably followed by an opposite feeling and mood of Depression, and moods and periods of Courage are succeeded by equal moods of Fear. Tides of feeling have ever risen and fallen with people, but they have never suspected the cause or reason for these mental phenomena.

An understanding of the workings of the Principle of Rhythm and the Law of Neutralization will give one the key to the Mastery of these rhythmic swings of feeling and will enable them to know themselves better and to avoid being carried away by these inflows and outflows.

The Will is superior to the conscious manifestation of this Principle, although the Principle itself can never be destroyed. We may be able to avoid its consequences, but the Principle remains in effect. The pendulum always swings, but we can avoid being carried along with it.

Therefore, the Hermetic approach to the Principle of Rhythm goes beyond what modern science has grasped. By understanding the Law of Neutralization, Hermetic Masters have found a way to rise above the swing of the pendulum and achieve a state of mental firmness and poise that is almost impossible for those who allow themselves to be tossed about by their moods and emotions. While the swings of Rhythm are an ever-present part of human mental activities, the Hermetic approach provides the key to the Mastery of these rhythmic swings of feeling and enables us to avoid being carried away by them. This understanding helps us to know ourselves better, gain self-mastery, and rise to the higher plane of consciousness. Through this understanding of the Principle of Rhythm, we can transcend the limitations of our lower mental states and achieve a state of mental poise and firmness.

The mastery of the Principle of Rhythm is a vital aspect of Hermetic philosophy and one that holds great importance for anyone seeking to attain self-mastery. The swings of the Rhythmic pendulum are a part of every person's life, and without an understanding of this Principle, we are at the mercy of our moods, feelings, and emotions.

The Hermetic Masters recognized that the swings of the Rhythmic pendulum occur on the unconscious plane of mental activity, and by raising our consciousness to the higher plane, we can escape its influence. The Law of Neutralization, which is the basis of this Principle, allows us to rise above the negative swings of the pendulum and maintain a state of mental balance and equilibrium.

The key to the mastery of the Principle of Rhythm lies in the power of the Will.

By polarizing ourselves at the desired pole and refusing to participate in the backward swing of the pendulum, we can stand firm in our polarized position and allow the mental pendulum to swing back along the unconscious plane. This requires a great deal of mental discipline and self-control, but with practice, it becomes easier to maintain this state of mental poise and to avoid being carried away by the inflows and outflows of our moods and emotions.

In conclusion, the Principle of Rhythm is a universal law that affects all aspects of our lives, including our mental activities. By understanding this Principle and applying the Law of Neutralization, we can gain self-mastery and rise to the higher plane of consciousness. The swings of the Rhythmic pendulum are a part of our lives, but we have the power to avoid being carried along with it. The mastery of this Principle is a key aspect of Hermetic philosophy and one that holds great importance for anyone seeking to attain self-mastery and mental poise.

As we delve deeper into the workings of the Principle of Rhythm, it is important to consider the Law of Compensation. This law is defined by the Hermetists as "to counterbalance," and is referenced in the Kybalion when it states, "The measure of the swing to the right is the measure of the swing to the left; rhythm compensates." The Law of Compensation operates on the Physical Plane in numerous ways, including the pendulum of a clock, the seasons, the tides, and all rhythmic phenomena. In essence, a swing in one direction is always balanced by a swing in the opposite direction, or to the opposite pole.

This Law is not limited to physical phenomena but also extends to mental states. The Hermetists teach that a person's capacity for pain and pleasure is balanced. The man who experiences intense joy must also suffer intense pain, whereas the man who feels little pain experiences little joy. Before someone can enjoy a certain degree of pleasure, they must have swung proportionately toward the opposite pole of feeling. The Negative is precedent to the Positive in this matter.

Therefore, pleasure is the Rhythmic swing, according to the Law of Compensation, for a degree of pain previously experienced either in the present life or a previous incarnation. This sheds new light on the Problem of Pain.

The Hermetists regard the chain of lives as continuous and forming part of one life of the individual. Therefore, the rhythmic swing is understood in this way and would be without meaning unless the truth of reincarnation is admitted. The process of Neutralisation allows the Master or advanced student to avoid the swing towards Pain to a large extent.

The Law of Compensation is a fundamental principle in the lives of both men and women. Everything has both positive and negative aspects. In general, one "pays the price" for whatever they own or lack. The rich have many things that the poor do not, and the poor frequently have things that the rich do not have. Even if several lives are required for the return swing of the Pendulum of Rhythm, the Law of Compensation is always in operation, striving to balance and counter-balance, and always succeeding in time.

In conclusion, the Law of Compensation is a powerful force that operates on both the physical and mental planes. It is a constant reminder that everything in life has its opposite, and a swing in one direction is always balanced by a swing in the opposite direction. By understanding this Law, we can gain insight into the Problem of Pain and learn to balance our own mental states. The Law of Compensation is a reminder that everything in life has a price, and that balance and harmony can only be achieved through the constant operation of this fundamental principle.

The Principle of Cause and Effect

"Every Cause has its Effect; every Effect has its Cause; everything happens according to Law; Chance is but a name for Law not recognized; there are many planes of causation, but nothing escapes the Law."—The Kybalion.

The Principle of Cause and Effect is a fundamental law that underpins the workings of the universe. It asserts that every effect has a cause, and every cause produces an effect. Nothing happens by chance, and everything unfolds according to laws and principles. The Hermetists have long understood this principle and have learned how to rise above the ordinary plane of cause and effect. By doing so, they become the causers instead of the effects. They play the game of life instead of being played by it.

Different planes of cause and effect exist, and the higher planes dominate the lower ones. However, nothing entirely escapes the law of cause and effect. The Masters, those who have achieved a high level of spiritual mastery, are able to rise to a higher plane where they dominate their moods, characters, qualities, and powers. They are not subject to the wills and desires of others, heredity, suggestion, or other outward causes. Instead, they become movers, using the principle of cause and effect to shape their reality.

The Principle of Cause and Effect reminds us of the interconnectedness of all things. Every event is the result of many factors coming together, and every action we take has an impact on the world around us. By being mindful of our thoughts, words, and actions, we can harness the power of cause and effect to manifest our desires and create the life that we want.

The Hermetists understand that the power of cause and effect extends beyond the physical plane, and that there are many planes of causation that influence the way events unfold. They know that by obeying the causation of the higher planes, they can help to rule on their own plane.

This knowledge allows them to become conscious creators of their own reality, using the principle of cause and effect to shape their lives and the world around them.

By studying and understanding the Principle of Cause and Effect, we can learn to take responsibility for the impact that we have on the world. We can become conscious creators of our own reality, using the power of cause and effect to manifest our desires and create a better world. This principle is not only a source of spiritual wisdom but also a practical tool that we can use to live more fulfilling lives. Let us all strive to understand and apply the Principle of Cause and Effect in our lives, for the benefit of ourselves and all beings.

Principle of Causation

The Principle of Cause and Effect is a fundamental concept that has underpinned scientific thought throughout history. This principle, first articulated by the Hermetic Teachers, has been accepted by virtually all world thinkers worthy of the title. It is the basis for understanding the natural world and the way in which it operates.

While there have been disagreements between various schools of thought, these disagreements have primarily concerned the details of the Principle's operations and the meaning of specific words. However, the underlying Principle of Cause and Effect has remained constant and correct. To believe otherwise would be to remove the universe's phenomena from the domain of Law and Order and place them under the control of the fictitious entity known as "Chance."

It is important to note that there is no such thing as pure Chance. The word "Chance" is merely an expression relating to obscure causes—causes that we cannot perceive, causes that we cannot understand. Webster defines the word "Chance" as "a supposed agent or mode of activity other than a force, law or purpose; the operation or activity of such agent; the supposed effect of such an agent; a happening; fortuity; casualty, etc." But when the matter is closely examined, it is seen that there can be no such agent as "Chance," in the sense of something outside of Law—something outside of Cause and Effect.

It is impossible to imagine something acting in the phenomenal universe that is independent of its laws, order, and continuity. Such a thing would be completely independent of the universe's orderly trend and thus superior to it. Nothing outside of The All can be imagined to be outside of the Law, and this is only because The All is the Law in and of itself. There is no place in the universe for anything other than and independent of Law. The presence of such Something would render all Natural Laws ineffective, plunging the universe into chaos and lawlessness.

Upon closer examination, it becomes clear that what we call "Chance" is simply an expression relating to obscure causes that we cannot perceive or understand. The word Chance is derived from a word meaning "to fall" (as the falling of dice), the idea being that the fall of the dice (and many other happenings) are merely a "happening" unrelated to any cause. But when the matter is closely examined, it is seen that there is no chance whatsoever about the fall of the dice.

When a die falls and displays a particular number, it obeys a law as unbreakable as the one that governs the revolution of the planets around the sun. Causes, or chains of causes, run back further than the mind can follow from the fall of the die. Causes include the position of the die in the box, the amount of muscular energy expended in the throw, and the condition of the table. But, behind these visible causes, there are unseen preceding causes, all of which had an impact on the number of the die that fell highest.

If a die is cast a great number of times, it will be found that the numbers shown will be about equal; that is, there will be an equal number of one-spot, two-spot, etc., coming uppermost. Toss a penny in the air, and it may come down either "heads" or "tails"; but make a sufficient number of tosses, and the heads and tails will about even up. This is the operation of the law of average. But both the average and the single toss come under the Law of Cause and Effect, and if we were able to examine the preceding causes, it would be clearly seen that it was simply impossible for the die to fall other than it did, under the same circumstances and at the same time. Given the same causes, the same results will follow. There is always a "cause " and a "because" to every event. Nothing ever "happens" without a cause, or rather a chain of causes. These chains of causation extend back into the past and forward into the future, forming an unbroken stream of cause and effect that permeates the entire universe. This stream of causation is what makes the universe an orderly and predictable place, and it is what allows us to make sense of the world around us.

The Principle of Cause and Effect is not just a theoretical concept, but a practical tool for understanding and manipulating the world. By understanding the causes that lead to a particular effect, we can take steps to reproduce that effect in a controlled and predictable manner. This is the basis of all scientific inquiry and technological innovation.

Despite its importance, the Principle of Cause and Effect is often misunderstood and misused. Many people believe in the existence of "pure chance" or "luck," as if events could happen without any underlying cause. Others may acknowledge the existence of causation but fail to recognize the complexity of the chains of causation that lead to a particular event. This can lead to oversimplifications and misunderstandings, such as assuming that a single cause is responsible for a complex phenomenon or failing to take into account all the contributing factors.

To truly understand the Principle of Cause and Effect, we must recognize that it operates at all levels of existence, from the smallest subatomic particles to the largest galaxies. Every event, from the formation of a star to the fall of a leaf, is the result of a complex web of causes and effects. By studying these causes and effects, we can gain a deeper understanding of the workings of the universe and our place within it.

As we explore the Principle of Cause and Effect, some individuals may find themselves perplexed by the idea of one thing causing another. How can one thing be the "creator" of another thing? In truth, no "thing" can cause or create another "thing." Cause and Effect is concerned solely with "events." An event is "that which comes, arrives, or happens, as a result or consequent of some preceding event." There is no creation of one event by another; instead, every event is a previous link in the long, orderly chain of events that flows from The All's creative energy.

This chain of events is marked by continuity between all preceding, subsequent, and consequent events, and there is a connection linking everything that came before and everything that follows.

Take, for example, a stone that is dislodged from a mountainside and crashes through a roof of a cottage in a valley below. At first glance, it appears to be a random occurrence, but on closer examination, we discover a vast web of causes behind it.

In the beginning, there was the rain, which softened the earth that supported the stone and enabled it to fall. Behind that was the influence of the sun, other rains, and so on, which gradually disintegrated the piece of rock from a larger piece. Then there were the causes that led to the formation of the mountain, and its upheaval by convulsions of nature, and so on, ad infinitum. We could go on to examine the causes behind the rain, and so forth. We could also examine the existence of the roof. In short, we would quickly become entangled in a labyrinth of cause and effect, from which we would try to free ourselves.

Similar to how a person has two parents, who in turn have four grandparents, eight great-grandparents, sixteen great-great-grandparents, and so on, until, for example, forty generations are calculated, the number of causes behind even the most insignificant event or phenomenon, such as the passage of a tiny speck of soot before your eye, becomes countless. Tracing the bit of soot back to its origins is no easy task, for it may have once been a part of a massive tree trunk that was eventually transformed into coal, and so forth, until it became the speck of soot that now passes before your vision on its way to other adventures. It took a mighty chain of events, causes, and effects to bring it to its current state, and this is only one event that will generate more events hundreds of years in the future.

Writing these lines was just one of the many events resulting from the tiny bit of soot, which caused the typesetter to perform specific tasks, the proofreader to do the same, and which will elicit certain thoughts in your mind and that of others, affecting still others, and so on, infinitely beyond man's capacity to comprehend—all from the passage of a tiny bit of soot. All of this illustrates the interconnectedness of things and the idea that "there is no great; there is no small; in the mind that causeth all."

Consider for a moment the possibility that the meeting of a certain man and a certain maid in the distant Stone Age was the ultimate catalyst for your very existence. It's a thought that may seem daunting at first, but it's worth contemplating. After all, if the couple who brought you into this world had never met, you wouldn't be here reading these lines today.

It's a fascinating concept that speaks to the interconnectedness of all things. Every thought, every action, every decision we make has a ripple effect that can influence the course of history. We are all part of a great chain of cause and effect, where the consequences of our choices can extend far beyond our immediate surroundings.

Of course, the question of whether we have free will or if everything is predetermined is one that has puzzled philosophers for centuries. The Hermetic Teachings suggest that both sides of the argument are partially true, and that the Principle of Polarity shows that both are but half-truths, opposing poles of truth. In other words, the truth lies somewhere in the middle.

For most people, the idea of true freedom is merely an illusion. They are slaves to their heredity, their environment, and the opinions of others. They are tossed about like a ship in a storm, unable to exercise any real control over their lives. But for the Master, things are different. The Master understands the rules of the game and is able to rise above the plane of material life. By placing themselves in touch with the higher powers of their nature, they are able to dominate their own moods, characters, and qualities, as well as their environment. They become Movers in the game, rather than Pawns - Causes instead of Effects.

Of course, this isn't to say that the Masters are immune to the laws of the universe. They simply understand how to work within them. They become a conscious part of the Law, rather than being mere blind instruments. While they Serve on the Higher Planes, they Rule on the Material Plane.

It's worth noting that extreme polar opposites are difficult to establish in most cases. The swing is always "towards" one pole and then the other. In all the airs and phenomena of the Universe, there is always action and reaction, advance and retreat, rising and sinking. This Principle is manifested in suns, worlds, men, animals, plants, minerals, forces, energy, mind, matter, and even Spirit. The Principle manifests itself in the creation and destruction of worlds, the rise and fall of nations, the life histories of all things, and finally in Man's mental states.

So the next time you find yourself pondering the mysteries of the universe, take a moment to consider the interconnectedness of all things. You may be surprised by what you discover.

The Principle of Gender

"Gender is in everything; everything has its Masculine and Feminine Principles; Gender manifests on all planes."—The Kybalion.

As we delve deeper into the mysteries of the universe, we come to realize that the forces of gender are present in all aspects of creation. From the tiniest subatomic particles to the vastness of the cosmos, the Masculine and Feminine Principles are always at work, shaping and influencing the world around us. The Principle of Gender is one of the fundamental principles of Hermeticism, and understanding its laws is crucial for unlocking the secrets of creation.

On the physical plane, the Principle of Gender manifests as sex, the interaction of male and female reproductive organs that is necessary for the continuation of the species. However, the principle goes beyond the physical and extends to the mental and spiritual planes, where it takes on higher forms. At its core, the Principle of Gender is always working towards generation, regeneration, and creation, and nothing in the universe can exist without its influence.

By recognizing and understanding the principles of gender, we can learn to harness the power of both masculine and feminine energy within ourselves and in our interactions with others. This can lead to greater balance, harmony, and creativity in all areas of our lives. Whether we are seeking to create something new or to regenerate something that has been lost, the Principle of Gender holds the key to unlocking our true potential.

However, it is important to note that the principle has nothing to do with the many base, pernicious, and degrading lustful theories, teachings, and practices that are taught under fanciful titles. These base revivals of the ancient infamous forms of Phallicism tend to ruin the mind, body, and soul, and the Hermetic Philosophy has always warned against these degraded teachings that lead to lust, licentiousness, and perversion of Nature's principles.

If one seeks such teachings, they must look elsewhere, as Hermeticism contains nothing for them along these lines. To the pure, all things are pure; to the base, all things are base.

Therefore, we must approach the Principle of Gender with reverence and respect, understanding that it is a powerful force that has the potential to unlock our highest potential. By studying and understanding this principle, we can learn to work with the natural laws of the universe, creating and regenerating in harmony with the forces of nature. The Principle of Gender contains the solution to many of the mysteries of life, and by embracing it, we can unlock the true potential of our being.

Gender

As we explore the intricate web of Hermetic philosophy, we inevitably come across the great Seventh Hermetic Principle, the Principle of Gender. This principle reveals a truth that transcends the physical plane and permeates every aspect of our existence. From the tiniest subatomic particles to the grandest cosmic phenomena, gender is present in all things, manifesting through the interplay of masculine and feminine principles.

It's essential to note that in Hermetic philosophy, gender and sex are not interchangeable terms. Sex refers solely to the physical distinction between male and female living things, whereas gender encompasses a much broader and more profound meaning. Derived from the Latin root meaning "to beget, to procreate, to generate, to create, to produce," gender is the force behind all creation, production, and generation.

However, it's worth noting that certain writers who have attempted to study Hermetic Philosophy have mistakenly associated the Seventh Hermetic Principle with various theories and teachings about sex that are often repugnant and fanciful. Thus, it's crucial to distinguish the difference between gender and sex when interpreting this principle correctly.

To understand the concept of gender in a scientific context, we must examine the corpuscles, ions, or electrons that make up the basis of matter. These tiny particles, by forming certain combinations, generate atoms, which were once believed to be indivisible. However, science has since discovered that atoms consist of a multitude of corpuscles, electrons, or ions revolving around each other and vibrating at a high degree of intensity.

The latest scientific findings suggest that the formation of atoms is due to the clustering of negative corpuscles around a positive one, where the positive corpuscles exert influence on the negative ones, causing them to assume specific combinations and generate or create an atom.

This aligns with the ancient Hermetic teachings that identify the masculine principle of Gender with the positive pole and the feminine principle with the negative pole of electricity.

It's essential to clarify that the public has an entirely erroneous impression regarding the qualities of the so-called "Negative" pole of electrified or magnetized matter. Science has wrongly applied the terms positive and negative to this phenomenon, and Hermetic philosophy warns us against this fallacy.

Understanding the Principle of Gender helps shed light on many subjects that have perplexed human minds, including the philosophy of mental and spiritual creation, generation, and regeneration. By recognizing the presence of both masculine and feminine principles within ourselves and in our interactions with others, we can harness their power to create greater balance, harmony, and creativity in all areas of our lives.

We must note, however, that the Principle of Gender is not a justification for base, pernicious, and degrading lustful theories, teachings, and practices that prostitute this natural principle. Hermetic philosophy has always warned against these degraded teachings that lead to lust, licentiousness, and the perversion of nature's principles. Only by seeking purity in all things can we hope to fully understand and benefit from the Principle of Gender.

In the study of electricity, the words "Positive" and "Negative" have been used for centuries to describe the two poles of a battery. However, recent scientific research suggests that these terms may be inadequate and misleading. The "Negative" pole, for example, is not actually negative in the sense of being weak or unreal. In fact, it is the source of all electrical phenomena, including the swarm of electrons that emerge from the cathode pole and the wonderful "rays" that have revolutionized scientific concepts over the last decade.

Given these new discoveries, it is no wonder that the best scientific authorities are now using the term "Cathode" instead of "Negative." The word Cathode is derived from a Greek root meaning "descent; the path of generation, etc." It is a much more accurate and descriptive term for the source of electrical energy and the place where new forms and energies are generated or produced.

The Cathode pole is the Mother of all the strange phenomena that have rendered useless the old textbooks and have caused many long-accepted theories to be relegated to the scrap-pile of scientific speculation. It is the Mother Principle of Electrical Phenomena, and of the finest forms of matter as yet known to science. This is why the old term "Negative" no longer does justice to the true nature of the Cathode pole. Instead, we should use the word "Feminine" in speaking of that pole of activity.

The latest scientific teachings suggest that the creative corpuscles or electrons are Feminine. While science says "they are composed of negative electricity," we say they are composed of Feminine energy. A Feminine corpuscle becomes detached from, or rather leaves, a Masculine corpuscle, and starts on a new career. It actively seeks a union with a Masculine corpuscle, being urged thereto by the natural impulse to create new forms of Matter or Energy. One writer goes so far as to use the term "it at once seeks, of its own volition, a union," etc. This detachment and uniting form the basis of the greater part of the activities of the chemical world.

When a Feminine corpuscle joins with a Masculine corpuscle, the process of ionization begins. Under the influence of Masculine energy, Feminine particles vibrate rapidly and circle around it. The outcome is the birth of a new atom. This new atom is actually made up of a union of Masculine and Feminine electrons, or corpuscles, but once formed, the atom becomes a separate entity with certain properties but no longer exhibiting the property of free electricity.

These unions or combinations manifest the varied phenomena of light, heat, electricity, magnetism, attraction, repulsion, chemical affinity and the reverse, and similar phenomena. And all this arises from the operation of the Principle of Gender on the plane of Energy. The Masculine principle seems to direct a certain inherent energy toward the Feminine principle, starting into activity the creative processes. But the Feminine principle is the one always doing the active creative work, and this is so on all planes.

Each principle is incapable of operative energy without the assistance of the other. In some forms of life, the two principles are combined in one organism. For that matter, everything in the organic world manifests both genders—there is always the Masculine present in the Feminine form, and the Feminine form in the Masculine. The Hermetic Teachings have long recognized this principle of Gender and its importance in the study of natural phenomena. As we continue to explore the mysteries of electricity, it is clear that a deeper understanding of Gender will be essential to unlocking its full potential.

The Hermetic Teachings delve into the operation of the two principles of Gender, which play a crucial role in the production and manifestation of various forms of energy. However, we must refrain from going into detail at this point, as we cannot back up our claims with scientific proof. Science has not yet progressed to the point where we can conclusively prove these teachings. Nevertheless, recent scientific discoveries show that science is on the right track, and the example of the electrons or corpuscles offers a general idea of the underlying principles.

Intriguingly, some leading scientific investigators believe that the formation of crystals corresponds to "sex-activity," which shows the direction in which scientific winds are blowing. With each passing year, new facts will emerge to confirm the Hermetic Principle of Gender's correctness. Gender operates continuously and manifestly in the field of inorganic matter and energy or force. Scientists now consider electricity the "Something" in which all other forms of energy appear to dissolve or melt.

The latest scientific doctrine, the Electrical Theory of the Universe, is gaining popularity and general acceptance. If we can detect Gender's unmistakable evidence and its activities, even at the root and source of electrical phenomena, we can conclude that science has finally offered proof of the great Hermetic Principle of Gender's existence in all universal phenomena. The attraction and repulsion of atoms, chemical affinity, the loves and hates of atomic particles, and the attraction or cohesion between matter molecules are all familiar phenomena that demonstrate the presence of the Gender Principle.

Have you ever considered that all of these manifestations are the result of the Gender Principle? Can't you see that the phenomenon is on all fours with corpuscles or electrons? Furthermore, can you not see the logic in the Hermetic Teachings that assert that the Law of Gravitation, that strange attraction that causes all particles and bodies of matter in the universe to gravitate towards each other, is simply another manifestation of the Principle of Gender? It attracts the Masculine to the Feminine energies, and vice versa. We do not have scientific proof of this at this time, but if you examine the phenomena in the light of the Hermetic Teachings, you will develop a better working hypothesis than any physical science has to offer.

Mental gender

In the field of psychology, the idea of the duality of mind has gained considerable attention in recent years. Several theories have emerged that attempt to explain the nature and composition of these "two minds." However, for students of Hermetic Philosophy, the concept of the duality of mind is not new. In fact, it has been a fundamental principle of this ancient wisdom tradition for centuries.

When examining the various modern theories regarding the duality of mind, Hermetic students may find themselves amused. Each school of thought tends to cling to its own ideas and claim to have uncovered the truth. However, a deeper investigation into the history of occult teachings reveals that the Hermetic doctrine of the Principle of Gender on the Mental Plane, which pertains to the manifestation of Mental Gender, has existed for thousands of years.

The idea of Mental Gender, which corresponds to the Masculine and Feminine Principles of Mind, can be easily understood by those familiar with modern theories of the duality of mind. The Masculine Principle is analogous to the Objective Mind, Conscious Mind, Voluntary Mind, and Active Mind. On the other hand, the Feminine Principle corresponds to the Subjective Mind, Subconscious Mind, Involuntary Mind, and Passive Mind.

However, it should be noted that the Hermetic Teachings do not necessarily agree with all modern theories on the nature of the two phases of mind. Some of these theories and claims may be far-fetched and incapable of standing the test of experimentation and demonstration. Nevertheless, the Hermetic Principle of Mental Gender offers an alternative perspective on the duality of mind, one that has been tested and refined over centuries of study and practice.

At first glance, it may seem like there is only an "I" existing within us. But upon closer examination, we realize that there is also a "Me" within us. These two mental constructs are distinct in their characteristics and nature, and understanding their interplay can shed light on many problems related to mental influence.

Let's begin with a consideration of the "Me." Many people mistake the "Me" for the "I" until they delve deeper into their consciousness. People tend to think of their "Me" as a collection of emotions, tastes, likes, dislikes, habits, peculiarities, and other characteristics that make up their personality. They are aware that these feelings are born, change, and eventually die away. They are also subject to the principles of Rhythm and Polarity, which can take them from one extreme of feeling to another.

Additionally, people consider the "Me" as a repository of knowledge that they have gathered throughout their lives. This knowledge forms a part of themselves. However, some people's "Me" is largely composed of their consciousness of their body and physical appetites. They identify so much with their physical nature that they practically "live there." Some people even consider their personal clothing as a part of their "Me" and see it as an extension of themselves.

According to one writer, "men are made up of three parts: soul, body, and clothes." These "clothes conscious" people would lose their personalities if they were stripped naked by savages during a shipwreck. Even those who are not as attached to their clothing still identify with their bodies as their "Me." They cannot imagine a Self apart from their bodies. In their view, their mind is practically "a something belonging to" their body.

However, as people become more self-aware, they can separate their "Me" from their idea of their body. They begin to think of their body as "belonging to" the mental part of themselves. Even then, they are prone to identify the "Me" entirely with their mental states, feelings, etc. They view these internal states as identical with themselves instead of merely being "things" produced by some part of their mentality.

As people continue to grow and develop, they can set aside various mental states, emotions, feelings, habits, qualities, characteristics, and other personal mental belongings. They learn to classify them in the "not-me" collection of curiosities and encumbrances, as well as valuable possessions. This requires a great deal of mental concentration and the power of mental analysis on the part of the student.

After this laying-aside process, the student finds themselves in conscious possession of a "Self" that can be considered in its "I" and "Me" dual aspects. The "Me" is felt as something mental that can produce thoughts, ideas, emotions, feelings, and other mental states. It can be considered as the "mental womb," capable of generating mental offspring. It reports to consciousness as a "Me" with latent powers of creation and generation of mental progeny of all sorts and kinds. Its creative energy is felt to be enormous, but it seems to require some form of energy from either its "I" companion or some other "I" before it can bring its mental creations into being.

This realization brings with it an enormous capacity for mental work and creative ability. However, the student soon discovers that this is not all that they find within their inner consciousness.

As the students delve deeper into the study of the mind, they discover a fascinating truth about themselves. They realize that there is a mental aspect within them that has the power to will their creative faculties into action. This same aspect can also step back and observe the mental creations that unfold. They refer to this part of themselves as their "I" and can consciously choose to reside in its consciousness at will.

The students come to understand that the "I" represents the masculine principle of mental gender, while the "Me" represents the feminine principle. The "I" embodies the aspect of being, while the "Me" embodies the aspect of becoming. The two aspects of the mind operate in a dualistic fashion, much like the principle of correspondence that operates on the grand plane of universal creation: "As above, so below; as below, so above."

The students become fascinated with the concept of mental gender, as it offers them a master key to the dimly lit regions of mental operation and manifestation. They come to appreciate that the feminine principle is the receptive one, always receiving impressions, while the masculine principle is expressive, always giving out or expressing.

The feminine principle is also responsible for generating new thoughts, ideas, and concepts, including the work of the imagination. Meanwhile, the masculine principle focuses on the work of the "Will" in its various forms. The students soon realize that without the active aid of the Will of the Masculine Principle, the Feminine Principle is prone to resting content with producing mental images that are the result of impressions received from the outside world, rather than generating original mental creations.

The students who can actively employ both principles in their mental operations and creations become highly successful in the field. They use the feminine principle for active mental generation and the masculine principle to stimulate and energize the creative portion of their minds. However, the majority of people rely very little on the Masculine Principle and are content to live according to the thoughts and ideas instilled in their "Me" from the "I" of other minds.

The students of psychic phenomena come across a host of fascinating phenomena, including telepathy, thought transference, mental influence, suggestion, hypnotism, and more. They find themselves seeking an explanation for these varied phases of phenomena, and many have turned to the theories of the various "dual mind" teachers. While these theories are not without merit, the students discover that the Hermetic Teachings regarding Vibrations and Mental Gender offer a more comprehensive explanation.

By understanding the principles of mental gender, the students come to see the two distinct phases of mental activity that are responsible for the many psychic phenomena they encounter.

They discover that the long sought-after key to unlocking these mysteries is within their reach. Armed with this knowledge, they can explore the world of psychic phenomena with greater insight and understanding.

The power of Mental Gender is a fascinating subject that sheds light on the way in which our thoughts and ideas are formed and influenced by others. As we have seen, the Masculine and Feminine Principles within our minds work in tandem to produce our thoughts and actions. In the case of Telepathy, we observe how the Masculine Principle projects its Vibratory Energy towards the Feminine Principle of another person, who then takes the seed-thought and allows it to grow and mature.

Similarly, Suggestion and Hypnotism work by directing the Masculine Principle of the person giving the suggestions towards the Feminine Principle of the other person. The recipient of the suggestion then accepts it as their own and begins to think and act accordingly. However, this process can be dangerous because the idea implanted in the recipient's mind may not be their own but rather a product of another's will.

Ideas thus implanted in the mind of another person can grow and develop, eventually becoming the person's rightful mental offspring, but they can also be like the cuckoo egg placed in the sparrow's nest, destroying the rightful offspring and making itself at home. The Masculine and Feminine Principles in a person's mind should coordinate and act harmoniously with each other. However, the Masculine Principle in the average person is often too lazy to act, resulting in them being ruled almost entirely by the minds and wills of others, who do their thinking and willing for them.

Few original thoughts or actions are performed by the average person, who is merely a shadow or echo of someone else with a stronger will or mind. This is because the average person dwells almost entirely in their "Me" consciousness and fails to realize that they have an "I" consciousness. As a result, they are polarized in their Feminine Principle of Mind, and the Masculine Principle, which is where the Will is located, remains inactive and unutilized.

The world's strong men and women invariably exhibit the Masculine Principle of Will, which is why their strength is materially dependent on this fact. Instead of living on the impressions made on their minds by others, they control their own minds with their Will, obtaining the desired mental images, and they also control the minds of others in the same way. Strong people manage to implant their seed thoughts in the minds of the masses, causing them to think in accordance with the desires and wills of the strong individuals. This is why the masses of people are such sheep-like creatures, never originating an idea of their own, nor using their own powers of mental activity.

The manifestation of Mental Gender can be observed all around us in everyday life. Magnetic persons are those who are able to use the Masculine Principle in a way of impressing their ideas upon others. Successful orators, actors, writers, preachers, and other people who are in the public eye are employing this principle to great effect. The peculiar influence exerted by some people over others is due to the manifestation of Mental Gender, along the Vibratorial lines above indicated. Personal magnetism, personal influence, and fascination, as well as the phenomena generally grouped under the name of Hypnotism, all derive their power from the principles of Mental Gender.

For those who have familiarized themselves with the phenomena generally spoken of as "psychic," the force of Suggestion plays a significant role. This force is the process or method whereby an idea is transferred to, or "impressed upon," the mind of another, causing the second mind to act in accordance therewith. The use of Suggestion is a powerful tool that can influence the thoughts and actions of others, making it a force to be reckoned with in the realm of Mental Gender.

To truly comprehend the various psychical phenomena that Suggestion underlies, one must have a correct understanding of Suggestion itself. However, it is not enough to stop there. A knowledge of Vibration and Mental Gender is also necessary for the student of Suggestion.

This is because the whole principle of Suggestion depends upon the principle of Mental Gender and Vibration.

Most writers and teachers of suggestion only explain that the "objective or voluntary" mind makes the mental impression or suggestion on the "subjective or involuntary" mind. Unfortunately, they do not describe the process or provide an analogy in nature that would help us better understand the concept. But if we look at the matter through the lens of the Hermetic Teachings, we can see that the energizing of the Feminine Principle by the Vibratory Energy of the Masculine Principle is in accordance with the universal laws of nature. In fact, the creation of the Universe follows this same law.

The Hermetic Teachings show us that in all creative manifestations on the planes of the spiritual, the mental, and the physical, there is always in operation this principle of Gender - this manifestation of the Masculine and the Feminine Principles. "As above, so below; as below, so above." The natural world provides countless analogies whereby this principle may be understood. Once the principle of Mental Gender is grasped and understood, the varied phenomena of psychology become capable of intelligent classification and study, instead of being shrouded in mystery.

The immutable universal laws of life form the basis of this principle, and it "works out" in practice. We will not delve into the many different aspects of psychic phenomena or mental influence in great detail here. Many books, some excellent, have been written and published on this subject in recent years. While the main facts in these books are correct, the authors have attempted to explain the phenomenon with their own pet theories.

The student can become familiar with these matters, and by employing the theory of Mental Gender, they will be able to bring order out of the chaos of conflicting theories and teachings. This can help them easily master the subject if they so desire.

The purpose of this work is not to provide an extended account of psychic phenomena, but rather to give the student a master key to unlock the many doors leading to the parts of the Temple of Knowledge they may wish to explore. Through a consideration of the teachings of The Kybalion, one may find an explanation that will clear away many perplexing difficulties - a key that will unlock many doors.

There is no need to go into detail about all of the many features of psychic phenomena and mental science, provided we place in the hands of the student the means to acquaint themselves fully with any phase of the subject that may interest them. With the aid of The Kybalion, one may go through any occult library anew, with the old Light from Egypt illuminating many dark pages and obscure subjects.

The law of use (Hermetic Axioms)

The possession of knowledge, if kept dormant and unexpressed, is akin to hoarding precious metals—a futile and foolish endeavor. Knowledge, much like wealth, is intended to be utilized and put into action. The universal law of use governs this principle, and those who disregard it suffer the consequences of their resistance against natural forces.

The Hermetic Teachings, although carefully safeguarded within the minds of their privileged custodians, were never meant to be mere treasures hidden away. The emphasis on the law of use resonates strongly in these teachings, as evident from the aforementioned quote from The Kybalion. Knowledge devoid of application and expression serves no purpose, benefiting neither its possessor nor the collective progress of humanity. It is essential to avoid the mentality of hoarding knowledge and instead employ what you have learned. Absorb the axioms and aphorisms, but above all, put them into practice.

Here are some of the profound Hermetic axioms from The Kybalion, accompanied by brief commentary on each. Make these principles your own and diligently apply and embody them, for they only become truly yours through practical utilization.

By consciously directing your attention toward a more desirable state, you can alter your mental vibrations. Will acts as the guiding force for attention, and through attention, vibrations can be transformed. Cultivate the art of attentive focus by employing your will, and you will gain mastery over moods and mental states.

To eliminate an unwanted mental vibration, utilize the principle of polarity and concentrate on the opposite pole of what you wish to suppress. By changing the polarity, you can nullify the undesirable vibration and ultimately eliminate it.

This represents one of the pivotal Hermetic Formulas, rooted in authentic scientific principles. We have previously revealed that a mental state and its contrary are merely two poles of the same entity. Through Mental Transmutation, these polarities can be reversed. This principle is acknowledged by modern psychologists who employ it to break undesirable habits, encouraging their students to concentrate on the opposite quality.

If fear has taken hold of you, do not waste time attempting to eradicate it directly. Instead, nurture the quality of courage within yourself, and fear will naturally dissipate. Some writers have vividly depicted this concept using the analogy of a dark room. You need not laboriously remove or sweep away the darkness; simply open the shutters and allow the light to flood in, and darkness will be vanquished. To eliminate a negative quality, focus on the positive pole of that very quality, and gradually, the vibrations will shift from negative to positive until you become polarized on the positive side instead of the negative. The reverse is also true, as many have painfully discovered when they incessantly aligned themselves with the negative pole of things. By altering your polarity, you can master your moods, transform your mental states, reshape your disposition, and forge your character. The adept Hermetics owe much of their Mental Mastery to the application of this principle of Polarity, which constitutes a crucial aspect of Mental Transmutation. Remember the Hermetic Axiom: "Mind (as well as metals and elements) may be transmuted from state to state; degree to degree; condition to condition; pole to pole; vibration to vibration."

The mastery of Polarization represents a profound understanding of the fundamental principles of Mental Transmutation or Mental Alchemy. One cannot influence their environment unless they learn to change their own polarity. Grasping this principle empowers one to alter not only their own polarity but also the polarities of others, provided they dedicate the necessary time, care, study, and practice to master this art.

The principle itself is accurate, yet the results one attains are contingent upon the student's perseverance and dedication to practice. Rhythm can be neutralized through the skillful application of the Art of Polarization.

In our preceding chapters, we have extensively elucidated the Hermetists' belief in the manifestation of the Principle of Rhythm not only on the Physical Plane but also on the Mental Plane. It is within the realm of the mind that the bewildering procession of moods, feelings, emotions, and various other mental states unfolds, all owing to the rhythmic swing of the mental pendulum. This pendulum carries us ceaselessly from one extreme of emotion to its opposite.

Additionally, the Hermetists impart teachings on the Law of Neutralization, which offers a means to overcome the influence of Rhythm in consciousness to a significant extent. As we have previously expounded, there exists a Higher Plane of Consciousness, transcending the ordinary Lower Plane. By mentally ascending to this elevated realm, the adept achieves a state where the swing of the mental pendulum manifests solely on the Lower Plane. By dwelling in this heightened consciousness, the adept transcends the awareness of the pendulum's backward motion. This remarkable feat is accomplished through the process of polarizing oneself on the Higher Self, thus raising the mental vibrations of the Ego beyond those of the ordinary plane of consciousness.

This analogy can be likened to rising above a phenomenon, allowing it to pass beneath one's elevated position. The adept Hermetist aligns themselves with the Positive Pole of their Being—the "I Am" pole rather than the pole of mere personality. By resolutely "refusing" and "denying" the operation of Rhythm, they elevate themselves above the plane of its influence, standing steadfast in their Statement of Being. In doing so, they permit the pendulum to swing back on the Lower Plane without altering their Polarity. Individuals who have attained varying degrees of self-mastery, regardless of their comprehension of the law, accomplish this feat.

They simply "refuse" to allow themselves to be swayed by the pendulum of mood and emotion. Through unwavering affirmation of their superiority, they remain polarized on the Positive pole. The Master, of course, attains an even greater level of proficiency due to their understanding of the law they are triumphing over with a higher law. Through the application of their Will, they achieve a degree of Poise and Mental Steadfastness that appears almost unbelievable to those who allow themselves to be tossed back and forth by the mental pendulum of fluctuating moods and feelings. It is crucial to remember, however, that in this process, the Principle of Rhythm is not truly destroyed, for it is inherently indestructible. Rather, one overcomes this law by counterbalancing it with another, thus maintaining equilibrium.

The laws of balance and counterbalance operate not only on the physical planes but also on the mental planes. Understanding these laws empowers individuals to seemingly overthrow laws while in reality exerting a counterbalancing force.

Indeed, nothing eludes the grasp of the Principle of Cause and Effect, yet it is vital to comprehend that there exist multiple Planes of Causation. By harnessing the laws of higher planes, one can surmount the laws of the lower planes.

Through a deep understanding of the practice of Polarization, the Hermetists ascend to a higher plane of Causation. In doing so, they skillfully counterbalance the laws that govern the lower planes of Causation. Rising above the realm of ordinary Causes, they assume the role of Causes themselves rather than being solely influenced by external forces. By mastering their own moods and feelings and neutralizing the influence of Rhythm, as we have previously discussed, they chart a course distinct from the masses. The masses, obedient to their environment, find themselves subject to the wills and desires of others more powerful than themselves, the effects of inherited predispositions, the suggestions of those surrounding them, and various other external causes that maneuver them like pawns on the vast chessboard of life.

Conversely, the advanced Hermetists strive to ascend to a higher plane of mental action by transcending these influencing causes. Through their mastery of moods, emotions, impulses, and feelings, they mold new characters, qualities, and powers, thus triumphing over their ordinary environment. In doing so, they transform from mere pawns into astute players in the game of life, armed with understanding and guided by the Principle of Cause and Effect rather than being subject to its sway.

By soaring above the plane of ordinary Causes, they adopt the role of Causes themselves, rather than being mere recipients of external influence. This ability allows them to evade a significant portion of the operations of Cause and Effect on the ordinary plane. Such mastery of self empowers them to create their own destiny, fashioning their lives with intention and purpose. These individuals, these masters of self, bear witness to the immense potential that lies within each of us to transcend the limitations imposed by external circumstances and become architects of our own fate.

The Law of Attraction and The Kybalion

The Law of Attraction, a captivating concept entwined with the New Thought movement and the realm of positive thinking, has gained remarkable popularity. It is often defined as the belief that our focused thoughts and emotions possess a vibrational frequency capable of attracting similar energy into our lives. Thus, whether our focus remains on positive or negative aspects, the Law of Attraction dictates that we draw corresponding experiences and people towards us.

This law finds itself intricately intertwined with the notion of manifestation—a process that brings our desires and intentions to fruition. Manifestation involves not only visualizing and feeling as though we have already achieved our desired outcome but also taking deliberate action towards that goal.

Critics of the Law of Attraction argue that it oversimplifies complex issues and may inadvertently lead to victim-blaming, as it suggests that individuals attract negative experiences solely through their own thoughts and emotions. However, proponents of this law perceive it as a potent tool for personal growth and transformation. By assuming responsibility for their thoughts and emotions, individuals can focus on consciously creating the life they genuinely desire.

Within the realm of the Law of Attraction, numerous words and expressions provide evidence of its influence. If you have ever used terms such as "out-of-the-blue," "fell into place," "serendipity," "synchronicity," "coincidence," "luck," "fate," "meant to be," or "karma," you have unwittingly acknowledged the workings of the Law of Attraction.

Comparisons are often drawn between the Law of Attraction and the Principle of Mentalism, one of the fundamental principles presented in the mystical work known as The Kybalion. This profound principle posits that the universe itself is a mental creation, existing within the expansive mind of the All—the universal consciousness.

Much like the Law of Attraction, the Principle of Mentalism asserts that our thoughts and emotions possess significant influence over our experiences and the nature of reality. According to this principle, we have the power to shape our experiences and reality by mastering our own thoughts and emotions and aligning them with the universal will.

While both the Law of Attraction and the Principle of Mentalism underscore the power of the mind in shaping experiences and reality, the Principle of Mentalism delves deeper by suggesting that the universe is not just influenced by the mind, but is, in fact, a mental creation. According to this perspective, everything that exists is a manifestation of the universal mind.

While the Law of Attraction primarily focuses on attracting positive experiences through positive thoughts and emotions, the Principle of Mentalism encompasses a broader scope. It implies that all experiences and reality are ultimately created and controlled by the universal mind. Thus, it highlights the importance of aligning our own thoughts and emotions with the will of the universe, emphasizing a connection to something greater than ourselves rather than solely pursuing positive experiences for personal gain.

While the Law of Attraction has garnered substantial attention for its assertion that thoughts and beliefs can attract positive or negative experiences into one's life, it has faced criticism for oversimplifying complex issues and placing excessive responsibility on individuals for their own misfortunes.

On the other hand, The Kybalion offers a more holistic perspective of reality—one that recognizes interconnectedness and the multifaceted nature of phenomena. Rather than attributing events solely to individual thoughts and beliefs, The Kybalion acknowledges the intricate web of factors that influence a situation.

The Kybalion draws extensively from the wellspring of Hermetic philosophy and other esoteric traditions, and its teachings have permeated many modern New Age and self-help movements. By encompassing a broader understanding of the world, The Kybalion's perspective allows for a nuanced exploration of interconnectedness and rejects the notion of placing undue blame or responsibility on individuals for their experiences.

The Science of the Law of Attraction

At the core of positive thinking and its profound impact on the Law of Attraction lies a physiological foundation rooted in the fundamental nature of energy. Energy, an omnipresent force, manifests in various forms, encompassing atomic, thermal, electromotive, kinetic, and potential energies. One of the fundamental principles guiding energy is its inherent indestructibility—energy can never truly be annihilated.

Delving into the intricate realm of matter, we discover that all matter consists of intricate arrangements of atoms. Each atom comprises a nucleus housing protons and neutrons, while electrons gracefully orbit the nucleus in predefined "orbitals" or energy levels, maintaining the atom's equilibrium. It is noteworthy that electrons possess the ability to ascend to "higher" orbits by absorbing energy or descend to "lower" orbits by releasing energy.

Remarkably, when atoms align themselves in a synchronous manner, a magnificent motive force emerges—a force in which all constituent elements harmoniously pull in the same direction. This phenomenon parallels the magnetization of metals through the alignment of their molecules, resulting in the creation of positive (+) and negative (-) poles—an incontrovertible reality grounded in the fabric of nature and science. It becomes evident that if physical laws governing quantifiable observations exist within one domain, it is highly probable that similar laws govern other domains, even if our current understanding fails to quantify them.

Thus, the Law of Attraction assumes a distinct guise—one stripped of fanciful notions or mystical allure. It stands as an intrinsic law—entwined within the very essence of your being—a law to which every atom within you perpetually responds, irrespective of your conscious awareness.

The Law of Attraction remains intimately connected to the vibrations emitted by your being. It seamlessly interacts with and amplifies the vibration you emit, be it positive or negative, offering forth an abundance aligned with your energetic frequency. In its simplicity, the Law of Attraction remains purely responsive to the intricate interplay of vibrations you emanate.

This intricate dance of energy and vibration forms the underpinnings of the Law of Attraction, intertwining the profound interplay between the physical and the metaphysical, the seen and the unseen. As we explore the depths of our existence, we come to realize that this captivating law operates at the very foundation of our being, shaping our experiences and weaving the fabric of our reality.

Non-deliberate Attraction

In the intricate tapestry of the Law of Attraction, a phenomenon known as Non-deliberate Attraction perplexes many seekers on their journey. Countless individuals find themselves repeatedly drawing negative experiences into specific areas of their lives, despite their belief in emitting only positive energy. Curiously, they remain unaware that their very act of observing their current circumstances unknowingly sets in motion a chain reaction, emitting a subtle yet potent negative vibe.

Consider the scenario where you cautiously open your wallet, only to confront the disheartening sight of emptiness. In that precise moment, a vibration permeates your being—a vibration resonating with lack, fear, or any other variant of negative energy. Even if this occurrence is not intentional, the Law of Attraction faithfully responds to the vibrational frequency you emit, thus presenting you with a mirrored reflection of your energetic state. Remarkably, this law does not discriminate between the actions that engender such negative vibrations. Whether you find yourself reminiscing, fantasizing, or merely observing, the Law of Attraction remains impartial in its response.

Thus, an intricate cycle of observation unfolds, imbued with profound significance:

You observe the manifestations and circumstances present in your life, spanning various realms such as finance, work, health, and relationships. This act of observation triggers the generation of a corresponding feeling or vibration, a force that can either be positive or negative in nature. Unbeknownst to many, this perpetuates the Observation Cycle—a cycle wherein the Law of Attraction dutifully responds to the vibration you emanate, thereby bestowing upon you a bounty that aligns with your energetic state, be it negative or positive.

It is crucial to recognize that the Law of Attraction permeates your existence, with or without your comprehension, appreciation, or faith in its existence. Whether you delight in the aspects you currently observe or harbor dissatisfaction, the Law of Attraction diligently operates, molding your reality in accordance with your vibrational frequency. Should you revel in the joys of your experiences, embracing them wholeheartedly, the Law of Attraction graciously endeavors to amplify their presence. However, should discontent and undesired circumstances plague your reality, it is then imperative to forge a deeper connection with the Law of Attraction—to engage in Deliberate Attraction.

At any given moment, you hold the power to discern the nature of the vibration you emit, whether it leans towards the positive or the negative. A simple introspection of the emotions swirling within you unravels the truth, for it is these very emotions that ignite the vibration within you. Within the ethereal realm of vibrations, only two classifications exist—positive and negative—each bearing the potential to shape your reality.

To transmute a negative vibration into one of positivity requires naught but a shift in the words you employ and the thoughts you entertain. Consider the simple inquiry, "So, what do I want?" As you traverse the realms of dialogue, shifting your focus from what you wish to avoid towards your desired outcome, a transformation takes place. The very fabric of your vibration alters, for you can emit only one frequency at a time. By modifying the tapestry of your words, a metamorphosis blossoms within, aligning your vibrational state with the harmony of positivity.

Thus, in the grand tapestry of existence, resetting your vibration necessitates naught but a recalibration of language and thought—a subtle yet profound realignment that unlocks the infinite potential of the Law of Attraction.

Within the grand tapestry of the Law of Attraction, time becomes an inconsequential factor in its meticulous workings. It pays no heed to the vibrations you once emitted five minutes, five days, five months, or even fifty years ago.

Instead, its unwavering focus rests solely on the vibrational frequency you currently radiate in this very moment. And in response, it proceeds to bestow upon you more of the same, magnifying the essence of your energetic offering.

When faced with an unwanted situation, the human inclination often veers towards the need for explanations—an instinctual urge to justify our presence in such circumstances. However, this compulsion to defend, rationalize, blame, or engage in the fruitless act of justification only serves to bind us within the realm of negative attraction. Each word spoken in an attempt to elucidate the reasons behind an undesirable reality perpetuates the very negative current we seek to escape. For how can one be focused on what they truly desire when their energy is entangled in explanations for their undesired experiences? Simultaneously entertaining both negative and positive aspects becomes an impossibility. Ironically, our fervent quest to pinpoint the origins of our troubles only prolongs our negative entanglement. Questions such as "What is the source of my troubles?" or "Why am I not where I want to be?" inadvertently hold us captive within the clutches of negative attraction. While it is natural to seek improvement and yearn for solutions, there exists a crucial distinction between earnestly pursuing resolutions and accentuating the need for a solution by incessantly highlighting the problem.

Recognizing that something falls short of our desires represents a pivotal initial step. However, the swiftness with which we redirect our attention towards seeking a solution determines our progress, for the vibrational frequency of a problem starkly contrasts with that of its solution. As we grow cognizant of the value inherent in the process of pivoting—shifting our focus from what is unwanted to what is desired—and become adept at swiftly identifying the undesirable, our ability to immediately direct our attention towards a solution intensifies. In doing so, we unveil a profound truth: our existence teems with an abundance of wonders, far outweighing the aspects that fall short of our desires.

Moreover, the daily utilization of the Book of Positive Aspects emerges as a powerful tool to foster a positive orientation. Gradually, it aids in tilting the balance of our thoughts towards what we genuinely seek. The more we devote our attention to seeking thoughts that elicit increasingly better feelings, the more evident the stark contrast between contemplating our desires and dwelling on their absence becomes apparent.

Should discomfort arise while speaking or contemplating improvements we desire—be it in our financial situation, relationships, or physical well-being—we must recognize that in that very moment, we impede our own progress. It is during such instances that the processes of pivoting and the Book of Positive Aspects extend their benevolent hands, guiding us to discern the subtle beginnings of our creative endeavors. Thus, we can swiftly release the negative entanglement and instead reach for the threads of positive thought.

Embarking on a journey from a thought that evokes a slight improvement in our well-being to subsequent thoughts that yield even greater contentment proves far more accessible than striving to leap directly to a state of sublime bliss. This is because all thoughts, all vibrations, fall under the influence of the Law of Attraction—its universal sway shaping our reality in ways profound and unseen.

To gauge the nature of the vibrations we emit, a simple examination of the results we manifest in various aspects of our lives suffices. These outcomes serve as a perfect reflection of the vibrational essence we project into the universe, a testament to the Law of Attraction's unwavering influence upon our experiences.

How to make the Law of Attraction work for you

To unlock the boundless potential of the Law of Attraction, one must embark on a profound journey of self-discovery and introspection. At the very core of this transformative odyssey lies the pivotal task of identifying your true desires. However, herein lies a paradoxical truth: while many individuals find themselves proficient in recognizing what they do not want, they often stumble when it comes to articulating their authentic aspirations. Yet, amidst this seemingly confounding situation, lies a glimmer of hope—a realization that knowing what you don't want can serve as a stepping stone towards manifesting your true desires.

In the realm of the Law of Attraction, contrast takes on an intriguing significance. It encompasses all that fails to resonate with your soul, inducing discomfort, dissatisfaction, or a sense of disharmony. When you encounter aspects of your life that evoke such negative emotions, the tendency to complain, discuss, or vehemently declare your aversion takes hold. Alas, in doing so, you inadvertently emit a negative vibration, thereby inviting the Law of Attraction to bestow upon you an amplified reflection of the very experiences you wish to avoid.

Yet, fear not, for within your grasp lies the key to transcend this cycle of unwitting attraction. It begins with granting your desires the undivided attention they deserve. By infusing them with positive energy, focus, and unwavering commitment, you elevate your vibrational frequency—a vital ingredient in the manifestation process. Merely identifying your desires is a mere fraction of the equation; it is through the deliberate act of bestowing them with attention that they seamlessly integrate into the tapestry of your current vibrational state.

The Law of Attraction dutifully aligns the stars of the universe to deliver unto you an abundance that mirrors the quality of your attention, energy, and focus. If you merely identify your desires but fail to devote your undivided attention, energy, and focus to them, their manifestation remains an elusive dream.

Thus, the crux lies in the ongoing dedication to nurturing your desires, allowing their vibration to harmoniously intertwine with your present energetic state. In this symphony of alignment, the Law of Attraction responds to the resonance you emit.

Regrettably, some individuals unravel the threads of their desires, meticulously listing their aspirations only to cast them aside, forgotten and neglected. They fail to recognize that the Law of Attraction operates solely on the canvas of attention. Indeed, manifestation flourishes when your focus becomes a devoted sanctuary for your desires.

They yearn for your unwavering attention, for it is through the magnifying lens of your conscious awareness that they come alive and materialize in wondrous ways. The Law of Attraction, ever the faithful servant, can only respond to that which you choose to embrace within the realms of your attention.

Therefore, dear seeker of dreams, take heed and nurture your desires with tender care. Give them the attention they crave and the energy they require to burst forth from the ethereal realms into the realm of tangibility. For it is through the alignment of your attention, energy, and focus that the dance of manifestation begins, culminating in a symphony of dreams transformed into reality.

Words of Affirmations

In the vast tapestry of manifestation, words possess a profound potency—an ability to shape the very fabric of our reality. Enter the realm of affirmations, a mighty tool harnessed by those seeking to wield the Law of Attraction in their favor. These potent statements, whispered in the present tense, serve as beacons of intention, declaring our desires to the universe. Yet, in the intricate dance of creation, it is crucial to grasp that the Law of Attraction responds not to the mere words we utter, but to the vibrations we emit, entwined with the emotions they evoke within us.

To unlock the full potential of affirmations, authenticity becomes paramount. Each statement must ring true within the chambers of your being, resonating with an undeniable sense of alignment. For when you speak untruths, doubt infiltrates your consciousness, birthing negative vibrations that reverberate through the energetic web of manifestation. Thus, it becomes imperative to refine your affirmations, imbuing them with a profound sense of truth and invigorating resonance.

A transformative path unfolds as you reframe your affirmations, infusing them with the enchanting essence of possibility. Begin each sentence with the words "I'm in the process of," effortlessly dissolving the barriers between your present reality and the grand tapestry of your desires. In this subtle linguistic shift, the fabric of truth intertwines with your being, igniting a symphony of authenticity that harmonizes with the Law of Attraction. True affirmations, aligned with your journey, evoke a resounding harmony of positive vibrations, setting the stage for miraculous manifestations.

Yet, dear traveler of dreams, affirmations are but one facet of the multifaceted diamond of deliberate attraction. Enter the realm of the Desire Statement—a trinity of purpose, carefully composed to amplify your vibrational frequency. This sacred composition consists of three elements, weaving together a symphony of intention.

It begins with an opening sentence, an invitation to the universe, beckoning it to witness the dance of your desires. The body, an exquisite tapestry of clarity drawn from the depths of your soul, infuses your vibrations with the hues of excitement, possibility, and hope. And finally, a closing sentence, a triumphant proclamation that seals your desires in the cosmic dance of creation.

Enveloped within the gentle embrace of affirmations and Desire Statements, you unlock the gateway to the Law of Attraction's majestic power. But tread mindfully, for authenticity and resonance are the sacred keys that unlock this cosmic dance. Let your affirmations be a reflection of your truth, kindling the fires of positive emotions within you. It is through these reverberating vibrations that the Law of Attraction finds its rhythm, aligning the stars to conspire in your favor.

Yet, even as the harmonious melodies of manifestation beckon, an insidious force lurks—a whisper of doubt, casting shadows upon the path to your desires. Limiting beliefs, those persistent echoes of negativity, imprison your dreams and sabotage your vibrational frequency. But fear not, for you possess the tools to transcend these shackles, liberating your consciousness and ushering forth the radiant light of your desires. Embrace the transformative power of thought, wielding it as a mighty sword to sever the chains of negativity. In doing so, you create space for the pure essence of allowing—a pivotal step in the grand tapestry of deliberate attraction.

Unshackle your dreams, dear seeker, by purging doubt and negative vibrations from your sacred sanctuary. Embrace the art of allowing, infusing your being with an unwavering belief in the manifestation of your desires. Remove the veils of uncertainty, and with a resolute heart, surrender to the cosmic currents that guide your journey. For in the realm of allowing, doubt finds no fertile ground, and the Law of Attraction dances gracefully to the harmonious rhythm of your unwavering faith.

With affirmations as your melodic hymn and the art of allowing as your guiding compass, venture forth on this transformative path of deliberate attraction. The cosmos eagerly awaits your arrival, ready to conspire in the wondrous tapestry of your dreams-turned-reality. Embrace the power within you, and let the symphony of manifestation unfold in magnificent harmony.

The principle of Kybalion and Alchemy

Alchemy, an ancient endeavor focused on converting base metals into gold and discovering the elixir of life, has long been connected to Hermeticism and the teachings of the Kybalion. In fact, one of the fundamental principles of the Kybalion is the principle of vibration, asserting that everything in the universe is in perpetual motion and that even the tiniest particles oscillate at varying frequencies.

This principle evokes the notion of the philosopher's stone in alchemy, which was thought to possess the ability to transmute base metals into gold and bestow immortality. The philosopher's stone was believed to emit a high frequency vibration, prompting alchemists to pursue it through a fusion of spiritual and scientific methods.

The Kybalion also places significant emphasis on mental alchemy, denoting the process of converting one's thoughts and emotions into positive and constructive forces. This concept closely aligns with the alchemical practice of transmutation, wherein alchemists aimed to transform their own consciousness and attain enlightenment.

Both the Kybalion and alchemy share a profound recognition of the interconnected nature of all things and uphold a belief in the potent capacity for transformation and transmutation.

The Alchemy

In the realm of esoteric knowledge, Alchemy emerges as a captivating discipline believed to have been birthed by a revered sage of ancient Egypt, Hermes Trismegistus. While shrouded in the mists of time, some Rosicrucian schools speculate that Hermes may have graced the world during the era of Moses and the Exodus of the Israelites. Alchemy, with its profound symbolism of fire and its connection to alchemical principles, is regarded as a fiery religion or philosophy. It carries within its essence the transformative power of transmutation and garners deep reverence and homage from those who delve into its secrets.

The principles of alchemy, so it is said, mirror the very principles Nature herself employs. Thus, alchemy is believed to have existed in the ethereal realms long before it descended to the earthly plane through the tutelage of enlightened Masters. A profound exploration of Nature's enigmatic tapestry reveals to the discerning student that the lofty Intelligences, the Elohim, and the Great Architect of the Universe, employed alchemical principles to manifest celestial bodies from the primordial chaos. This Cosmic Root Substance, known as "Sunyata" in the parlance of Buddhism, acted as a crucible for the alchemical dance of creation.

Alchemy, an ancient practice that seamlessly blends elements of science, philosophy, and spirituality, stands as a testament to human fascination with the transcendent. Its lofty purpose lies in empowering individuals to embark on a profound journey of self-transformation and catalyzing positive change within the world. Through a vast array of techniques, such as transmutation and precipitation, alchemy endeavors to mold the very fabric of matter, raising its vibrational frequency to a state of heightened perfection. Furthermore, it seeks to unravel the veiled truths and profound mysteries of the universe, illuminating the path to spiritual enlightenment and heightened consciousness for those who dare to embrace its teachings.

At the core of alchemy lies an ardent pursuit of understanding and harnessing the fundamental principles of creation and transmutation. This noble endeavor, intertwined with the welfare of humanity, beckons individuals towards self-realization and the transcendence of their limitations. As a multidimensional discipline, alchemy has long relied on veiled language and intricate symbols to impart its wisdom, for it arose during a time fraught with ecclesiastical persecution, desperately vying for recognition as a sacred system of spiritual development. Only in recent centuries have the existence of enlightened Masters within the secret brotherhoods of alchemy been unveiled to the wider public.

Within the realms of alchemical teachings, initiates were guided on a transformative journey, striving to transmute themselves into divine beings through the diligent application of yogic practices. This alchemical odyssey encompasses four distinct levels: the physical, the biological, the psychological, and the transcendental. While modern chemistry may dismiss alchemy as a mere pseudo-science, pioneers in the realm of quantum physics are beginning to contemplate the profound resonance between alchemical ideas and their own groundbreaking discoveries.

Physical alchemy, one of the three categories of alchemy, focuses on the transformation of substances, such as base metals, into gold. This aspect of alchemy has been exploited by many scams and charlatans who have claimed to have achieved transmutation. However, aspirants of Ancient Wisdom understand that true happiness cannot be found in material possessions and strive instead for truth and eternal knowledge. While the search for a universal panacea to cure human suffering is a noble desire, it is important to note that profit-driven motives can also drive this search. Nonetheless, there are contemporary alchemists who claim to have successfully accomplished transmutation in their laboratories.

Biological alchemy, the second category of alchemy, focuses on the rejuvenation of the physical body and the search for an "Elixir of Life" that would prolong human existence and provide immunity against diseases.

Initially, alchemists looked towards herbalism for plants that possessed the traditional virtues of the fabled "Fountain of Youth." For example, the Hindu mystics attribute such qualities to the "Soma" creeper, the Chinese Taoists declare that a certain mushroom called "lung chih" has the virtue of regenerating the physical body, and the Egyptian god Thoth is said to have described a life-giving mushroom that conferred immortality. However, alchemists later realized that the real Elixir of Life lied within themselves and had to be manufactured via psycho-biological means.

The search for the Elixir of Life thus gave way to the development of the third category of alchemy: psychological or mental alchemy. This category focuses on the development and refinement of the mind and its faculties, such as concentration, imagination, reasoning, mental quietude, and visualization. The ultimate goal of mental alchemy is to accelerate the process of evolution so that the mental body becomes fully developed, allowing the Ego and the waking consciousness to function fully in the mental realm.

Before making quick progress in developing these mental faculties, it is crucial to purge the mind of negative emotions and thoughts, such as phobias, neurosis, guilt, and resentments. The aspirant is advised to forgive both themselves and others and follow the steps of conviction, contrition, confession, consecration, and communion for spiritual unfoldment. Another vital step in mental alchemy is the unification of the male and female aspects of the psyche, which psychoanalysis has only touched the surface of.

However, mental alchemy is not considered the ultimate goal of alchemy but rather a stepping stone leading to transcendental alchemy, which is the ultimate goal of alchemy. Transcendental alchemy aims to raise humanity from a state of death to a state of grace by reuniting the disciple in full awareness with the Atma and, eventually, with the Monad. The realization of one's true identity and reality, as well as the expansion of human consciousness to embrace cosmic consciousness, results from this unio mystica, or mystical union, with the Absolute.

The Jivanmukta, or liberated being, is free of ignorance, maya, and mortality and shines with the radiance of the Sun.

Transcendental alchemy, like the previous categories of alchemy, is not a one-size-fits-all system of spiritual unfoldment. Instead, it caters to the different temperaments of individuals. Essentially yogic in nature, transcendental alchemy stresses meditation, concentration, and contemplation. The work of the previous levels of transmutation is also conducive to its successful outcome. It is through the pursuit of transcendental alchemy that one can achieve the ultimate goal of alchemy: the elevation of the human spirit from mere mortality to the radiance of the Sun.

Steps in Alchemy

Every spiritual system embarks on a profound journey of transformation, characterized by a series of steps or phases of development. Just as the Qabalist finds guidance in the fruits and paths of the sacred "Tree of Life," Mahayana Buddhism teaches its adherents about the various "bhumis," or "grounds," they must traverse. Sufism and Yoga also illuminate the rungs of the spiritual ladder, while Freemasonry's 33 degrees mirror the vertebrae of the human spine, with Kundalini ascending 33 rungs to reach the sahasrara chakra. Even the ancient Patriarch Jacob received a vision illustrating the ascent of a spiritual ladder.

In the mystical realm of alchemy, the number of stages required varies, with adepts proposing 5, 7, 9, 12, or even 14 steps. In this chapter, we shall explore the seven steps that form the foundation of alchemical transformation:

Step 1: Sanctification - This crucial first step involves the act of consecration, of rendering an object holy. Similarly, on the spiritual path, it entails committing one's life to an occult or esoteric purpose and objective. Like the wise men Kaspar and Melchior who followed the Star despite obstacles, the aspirant undertakes sanctification with unwavering determination.

Step 2: Purification - Through strict adherence to a spiritual and ethical code, the alchemist initiates the process of purification. This discipline uplifts the vibratory rates of atomic structures within the lower components of the self. Simultaneously, it disperses foul matter and toxins that corrupt the sheaths, preventing the entombment of the soul by heavy atoms. Purification unfolds within the tripartite principles of atomic elevation, foul matter dispersion, and prevention of densification.

Step 3: Putrefaction - Advancing from the previous stages, the alchemist enters a phase of putrefaction, intensifying the transformative process.

Through the holy fire, astral and mental toxins are cleansed from the spiritual structure, disintegrating the effluvia that parasitically feed on one's fears and ignorance. This stage serves as the foundation for the transmutation of the tomb-like state into a sacred temple. Just as a Freemason constructs a temple not made with hands, the alchemist focuses on internal metamorphosis, decomposing habitual thoughts and emotions that lack the quality of an Ascended Master.

Step 4: Fermentation - Emerging from the transformative crucible of putrefaction, the alchemist undergoes fermentation, symbolized in Christian mysticism by the Passion and the agonizing experience of Jesus at Gethsemane. Psychologically, this phase is marked by intense psychic activity, where doubts assail one's deepest convictions and beliefs, challenging them at their very core. Chemically, fermentation breaks down complex compounds, transforming them into new structures with the aid of an agent such as yeast.

Step 5: Combustion - Having weathered the "Dark Night of the Soul" in the previous stage, the alchemist now faces an even greater test: the "Dark Night of the Spirit." During this arduous phase, one may feel forsaken and severed from the source of being, lacking encouragement, inspiration, and support from teachers and loved ones. This trial demands the alchemist's utmost strength and resolve.

Step 6: Regeneration - At the heart of all religions lies the fundamental quest for regeneration, the laying of foundations for the transformative process of spiritual rebirth. It is through esoteric practices that one activates the regenerative phase of spiritual development, forging a direct connection with higher forces and principles. The alchemist becomes an active participant in the process of personal and collective rejuvenation.

Step 7: Atonement - Exoterically, atonement refers to the reparation of wrongs or injuries committed against others. Esoterically, it embodies the "unio mystica," the profound oneness between Man and God. Atonement signifies the ascension in which Man reunites with their "I AM Presence."

This marks the culmination of the path of human salvation and the attainment of alchemical gold. Through countless tests, trials, and initiations, the Seed of the Tree of Life planted in Man's Edenic consciousness matures, bearing the fruit of divine qualities. The ascent into the Light is the result of personal effort and labor, distinguishing the Master soul from the immature human being who relies solely on the merits and endeavors of others.

Thus, the alchemical journey, with its intricate and transformative steps, guides the seeker toward the ultimate realization of spiritual transcendence. It is a path of self-discovery, growth, and evolution, leading to the awakening of the divine potential within.

The Interwoven Paths: Alchemy and The Kybalion

Within the vast tapestry of spiritual knowledge, two intricate threads emerge, weaving together in a harmonious dance: alchemy and The Kybalion. These profound disciplines converge in their shared pursuit of transmutation, the transformative process that extends beyond the physical realm to encompass the mental and spiritual domains. As we embark on this exploration, we shall witness the intercessions between these ancient traditions, delving into their foundational principles and illuminating the path towards spiritual perfection.

At the heart of both alchemy and The Kybalion lies the essence of transmutation. Whether working with base metals, thoughts, or souls, the alchemist's alchemical artistry seeks to transmute the impure into the noble, the coarse into the refined. Guided by the wisdom of The Kybalion, practitioners draw upon the universal principles that underpin both disciplines, shaping their transformative endeavors.

The seven Hermetic Principles, intricately woven into the fabric of The Kybalion, stand as pillars of understanding and guidance, resonating harmoniously with the essence of alchemy. Within these principles, the Principle of Mentalism reveals the power of the mind, while the Principle of Correspondence unveils the interconnectedness of all things.

The Principle of Vibration demonstrates the rhythmic dance of energy, while the Principle of Polarity illuminates the dynamic interplay of opposing forces. Enshrined within the Principle of Rhythm is the understanding that all existence unfolds in pulsating cycles, while the Principle of Cause and Effect emphasizes the profound consequences of our actions.

Finally, the Principle of Gender speaks to the ever-present duality within creation, embodying the complementary aspects of masculine and feminine energies. Alchemists and disciples of The Kybalion alike embrace these principles as a guiding light, shaping their transformative endeavors with purpose and wisdom.

Central to the journey of both alchemy and The Kybalion is the profound significance of inner work. As seekers traverse the labyrinthine corridors of self-discovery, they embark on a sacred quest of purifying the mind, nurturing spiritual qualities, and unveiling the dormant virtues within. Compassion, wisdom, and love intertwine as the alchemist's inner crucible, forging the transformative fires that transmute the leaden aspects of the self into golden radiance. Alchemy and The Kybalion teach that this inner alchemy is not a mere indulgence but an essential foundation upon which transmutation can manifest.

Within the vast cosmos of universal laws, alchemists and Kybalion practitioners discover the ever-present orchestration of divine harmony. Immutable and transcendent, these laws govern both the physical and spiritual realms, revealing the inherent interconnectedness of all existence. Alchemists seek to unravel the mysteries of these laws, partnering with the cosmic symphony to manifest their intentions. Guided by The Kybalion, disciples delve into the profound wisdom held within these universal laws, aligning their actions and consciousness with the grand design of the universe.

Ultimately, alchemy and The Kybalion converge upon the radiant horizon of spiritual perfection. This sacred goal beckons practitioners to embark on a transformative odyssey of soul purification, transcending the limitations of the mortal realm. Through the crucible of inner alchemy, the alchemist's soul sheds its impurities, awakening to a higher level of consciousness. A symphony of divine harmony reverberates within the heart of the Kybalion disciple, resonating with the truth of their interconnectedness with the divine. Spiritual perfection is the radiant tapestry woven by alchemy and The Kybalion, a tapestry that reveals the inherent unity between humanity and the cosmic forces that shape existence.

The Kybalion and Quantum Physics

In the vast realm of knowledge, two seemingly disparate realms converge, unveiling intriguing similarities: The Kybalion and Quantum Physics. Though they arise from different domains, they share profound insights into the nature of reality and the role of the observer.

At the core of Quantum Physics lies a fundamental principle—the observer's influence on the observed reality. Similarly, The Kybalion imparts the wisdom that the mind is the architect of reality, emphasizing the observer's pivotal role in shaping the world. The Hermetic principle of Mentalism resonates with this notion, proclaiming, "All is mind; the universe is mental."

Embedded within The Kybalion, the Principle of Mentalism stands as a cornerstone of Hermetic philosophy. It declares the fundamental mental nature of the universe, positing that every aspect of existence, including physical matter, is the product of mental processes.

According to this principle, the Mind of the All—the universal consciousness permeating all—creates and sustains everything in the universe. Infinite and eternal, this universal consciousness is the wellspring of creation and sustenance.

Moreover, this principle illuminates the profound impact our thoughts and beliefs wield over our lives and the world around us. By wielding mastery over our thoughts and beliefs, we become architects of our reality, manifesting the life we desire. Here, the Law of Attraction emerges, asserting that our thoughts and beliefs attract corresponding experiences into our lives.

The Principle of Mentalism underscores the power of the mind and the significance of comprehending and harnessing this power to sculpt our desired reality.

With the Mental Nature of the Universe established, this principle elucidates the myriad mental and psychic phenomena that captivate public attention. Without such an understanding, these phenomena remain enigmatic, resisting scientific scrutiny. Grasping this profound Hermetic principle of mentalism empowers individuals to comprehend the laws governing the mental universe, nurturing personal well-being and advancement.

By possessing the Master Key, students unlock the myriad chambers of the mental and psychic temple of knowledge, traversing them with discernment and ease. This principle unveils the true nature of "Energy," "Power," and "Matter," highlighting their subservience to the mastery of the mind.

Long ago, one of the ancient Hermetic Masters scribed, "He who grasps the truth of the Mental Nature of the Universe is well advanced on The Path to Mastery." These words resonate as profoundly today as they did when first written. Without this Master Key, Mastery remains elusive, and the student's knocks echo in vain against the temple's numerous doors.

Quantum Physics introduces another intriguing concept: entanglement, where two particles become inexplicably linked, their states dependent on each other, irrespective of distance. This echoes the Hermetic principle of Correspondence, proclaiming, "As above, so below; as below, so above." In essence, everything in the universe interconnects, reflecting harmonious patterns across different scales.

Another profound concept, the principle of Correspondence, proclaims the existence of a harmonious correspondence between the laws and phenomena of the multifaceted planes of existence and life. "As above, so below; as below, so above." Within this principle lies the revelation that the laws governing the physical universe extend their reach to the realms of the mental, emotional, and spiritual. All planes of existence are intricately interwoven, bound by a symphony of shared laws and principles.

Parallel echoes reverberate within the realm of modern physics, unveiling the concept of a holographic universe. According to this theory, the universe itself is a hologram, wherein each fragment contains the entirety of cosmic information. Mirroring this notion, the principle of Correspondence suggests that every plane of existence harbors insights into all others, encapsulating the very essence of shared governance.

Yet, the principle of Correspondence extends far beyond theoretical realms, offering practical applications in our daily lives. Through its understanding, we gain the ability to discern patterns and interconnections amid seemingly disparate events. We unlock the door to comprehending the intricate dance between our thoughts, emotions, and actions, and their repercussions across all levels of existence. Armed with this profound knowledge, we become catalysts for positive transformation, shaping our reality with intention.

Universally applicable and manifesting across the vast tapestry of the material, mental, and spiritual universe, this principle stands as an unwavering universal law. Ancient Hermetists revered it as one of the most potent mental tools, empowering individuals to transcend obstacles and glimpse the enigmatic beyond. Through its utilization, a glimpse of the veiled countenance of the goddess Isis became possible. Just as the mastery of geometric principles enables man to measure distant suns and trace their celestial paths from the observatory, the understanding of Correspondence empowers us to traverse the realms of the known and reason intelligently toward the unknown.

With each revelation, the seeker's understanding deepens, drawing closer to the enigmatic unity that underlies the tapestry of existence. Through Correspondence, the threads that bind the cosmos are unveiled, guiding us toward a profound comprehension of the interconnectedness that permeates all.

Interesting is the interplay between Quantum Physics and the Kybalion. Quantum Physics, with its resplendent revelations, affirms the interchangeability of matter and energy, as immortalized in Einstein's iconic equation, $E=mc^2$. Mirroring this, the Kybalion imparts its ancient wisdom, teaching us that all that exists is composed of vibratory energy, with matter representing a denser manifestation of this ethereal dance. Anchored within the Hermetic principle of Vibration, it declares, "Nothing rests; everything moves; everything vibrates."

Within the grand symphony of existence, remarkable parallels emerge, binding the realms of the scientific and the esoteric. The truths they unveil resonate with undeniable harmony, illuminating the integral role of the observer in shaping the world around them. Though their paths may diverge, their shared principles beckon us toward a profound understanding of the fabric of reality.

In the sanctum of Hermetic philosophy, the Principle of Vibration holds its place among the seven pillars of wisdom, enshrined within the pages of the Kybalion. It proclaims that the entire cosmos is perpetually in motion, every facet pulsating with vibrant energy at varying frequencies. From the celestial realms to the depths of our consciousness, all is woven together by the eternal rhythm of these sacred vibrations.

According to this profound principle, the interconnectedness of existence knows no bounds. It transcends the barriers that separate the physical, mental, and spiritual planes, bridging them effortlessly through the medium of vibratory energy. This sublime dance shapes the very essence of matter and energy, orchestrating the symphony of creation throughout the cosmos.

In the annals of scientific inquiry, the echoes of this timeless wisdom resound within the study of quantum mechanics and the intricate ballet of subatomic particles. Modern science, too, acknowledges that all matter is composed of minuscule particles vibrating in perpetual interplay, each influencing the other with its energetic cadence.

Yet, the Principle of Vibration reaches far beyond the boundaries of empirical inquiry. It extends its ethereal tendrils into the realms of the metaphysical, beckoning seekers to contemplate the profound nature of vibrations and their profound impact on the tapestry of existence. Within its luminous embrace lies the key to unraveling the enigmas of the universe—the interconnectedness of all things and the transformative power of shifting our vibrational frequencies. By harmonizing our thoughts and emotions with the celestial rhythm, we wield the ability to shape our own reality.

As we delve deeper into the heart of matter, science unravels its enigmatic secrets. Matter and energy, intertwined in the cosmic waltz, reveal themselves as forms of vibratory motion. Minds, too, emerge as a melodic expression of this ethereal dance. Science, with its unwavering gaze, unveils the ceaseless vibration that pulses through all matter, transcending temperature and defying stillness. From the subatomic realm to the cosmic expanse, the ceaseless dance of atoms and celestial bodies alike unfolds—a symphony of perpetual motion.

Yet, as the symphony of existence plays on, there remain mysteries unexplained. Science, for all its strides, has yet to fathom the nature of Cohesion—the invisible thread that binds molecules—and Chemical Affinity—the captivating force that binds atoms. And Gravitation, that celestial embrace that unites every particle and mass, continues to elude our complete understanding.

The cosmic dance of vibrations reveals a realm where science and ancient wisdom converge. It invites us to venture beyond the veil of the known, daring to explore the profound mysteries that lie at the threshold of human comprehension. Through the lens of Correspondence, we glimpse the interconnectedness of the realms, the harmonious symphony that resonates through every fiber of existence. Within this cosmic ballet, the seeker finds solace and inspiration, gazing upon the intricate choreography that shapes the very fabric of our reality.

The Kybalion and Modern Spirituality

The profound impact of the Kybalion on modern spirituality, particularly within the New Age movement, cannot be overstated. Its timeless principles, such as the Law of Attraction and the transformative power of positive thinking, have permeated the realms of self-help and personal development, resonating with countless individuals on their spiritual journeys.

In this ever-evolving landscape of modern spirituality, there is a shared yearning for a deeper connection—an intangible energy that surpasses the confines of the physical and mental realms. Across various spiritual traditions, meditation emerges as a unifying practice, serving as a pathway to forge a profound spiritual bond.

Modern spirituality embraces a vast tapestry of beliefs, practices, and traditions, reflecting the beautiful diversity of human experiences. At its core, it is characterized by an unwavering focus on personal spiritual growth, the quest for self-realization, and a deep appreciation for inner exploration. With a foundation built upon meditation, mindfulness, and holistic well-being, it embraces the harmonious integration of mind, body, and spirit.

This multifaceted movement draws inspiration from an array of traditions and practices, transcending cultural and geographical boundaries. Eastern spirituality, Western esotericism, indigenous wisdom, and New Age movements intertwine in a rich tapestry of influences. Ancient wisdom teachings, modern psychology, neuroscience, quantum physics, and alternative healing modalities converge, offering a vast wellspring of knowledge and insight.

In the realm of modern spirituality, the practices of mindfulness and meditation shine with resplendent clarity. Mindfulness, a state of heightened awareness and presence, becomes a sacred doorway to the present moment.

By immersing oneself fully in the unfolding tapestry of experiences, free from judgment and distraction, mindfulness gifts us with reduced stress, enhanced mental clarity, and an overall sense of well-being.

And then there is meditation, a cherished technique that beckons us to quiet the mind and embark on a journey inward. Through gentle contemplation and focused attention, we find solace in silence. Whether it be the rhythm of the breath, a chosen word, or a captivating image or sound, meditation guides us to a profound state of relaxation. This timeless practice, carried through the annals of history, showers us with immeasurable benefits—easing anxiety and depression, enhancing sleep, and evoking an inner joy and contentment. And in its essence, meditation aligns with the principle of mentalism, where the power of attraction finds its roots in the fertile soil of our thoughts and intentions, birthing them into tangible reality.

The principle of mentalism finds its reflection in the interconnected tapestry of the universe—a cosmic dance of energy and consciousness. The principle of correspondence whispers the ancient wisdom of "as above, so below," reminding us of the seamless bond that unites all things. It is the silent thread that weaves the fabric of our existence, inviting us to honor the intricate interplay of the universe. The principle of vibration, resonating with the eternal rhythm of existence, declares that change is the only constant. It reminds us that everything dances in perpetual motion, from the smallest atoms to the grand celestial bodies.

In the symphony of modern spirituality, the Kybalion's teachings reverberate with timeless wisdom. They find resonance with the law of attraction, mindfulness practices, and the transformative art of meditation. Their influence extends beyond the boundaries of individual belief systems, inspiring esoteric and mystical traditions such as Hermeticism and Thelema.

For those traversing the path of spiritual growth and enlightenment, the Kybalion's principles offer guidance and illumination. They nurture our understanding of the intricate workings of the universe and our unique place within its cosmic embrace. With open hearts and curious minds, we embark on a transformative journey, propelled by the profound wisdom that echoes through the ages.

Yoga, Spirituality and Kybalion

Yoga, a practical system of self-culture, stands as an exact science that seeks the harmonious development of body, mind, and soul. Through the profound practice of Yoga, one learns to turn their senses away from the external world and direct their focus within. It is a transformative journey that leads to eternal life in the soul or spirit, aiming to gain mastery over the mind and its fluctuations.

Embarking on the path of Yoga is an inner pilgrimage that commences at the very core of your being—the heart. It serves as a discipline for the mind, senses, and physical body, harmonizing and harnessing the subtle forces that reside within. As one delves deeper into the practice of Yoga, they discover the essence of perfection, peace, and everlasting happiness. Its benefits extend beyond the mat, permeating into the realms of daily life and business, granting calmness of mind, restful sleep, increased energy, vigor, vitality, longevity, and an elevated standard of health.

Yoga possesses the remarkable ability to transmute our animal nature into a divine one, elevating us to the pinnacle of divine glory and splendor. By engaging in the practice of Yoga, one gains the power to control their emotions and passions, thus fostering the strength to resist temptations and eradicate disturbing elements from the mind. A balanced and serene mind emerges, casting away fatigue, while offering a resolute focus and concentration. Through the profound practice of Yoga, communion with the divine becomes attainable, guiding practitioners towards the ultimate fulfillment of existence.

Within the vast realm of Yoga, various paths unfold, each with its unique focus and approach, catering to the diverse needs and inclinations of individuals.

Some of the most widely embraced types of yoga include:

1. Hatha Yoga: This is the most prevalent form of yoga practiced in the Western world. It emphasizes physical postures (asanas) and breathing techniques (pranayama) to enhance physical strength, flexibility, and relaxation.
2. Kundalini Yoga: Kundalini yoga seeks to awaken the dormant energy at the base of the spine and channel it upward through the chakras, the body's energy centers. It incorporates physical postures, breathing techniques, chanting, and meditation.
3. Bhakti Yoga: Focusing on devotion and worship of a personal deity, Bhakti Yoga finds expression through the chanting and singing of devotional songs (bhajans) and prayers.
4. Jnana Yoga: Jnana yoga, the path of knowledge and wisdom, places emphasis on self-inquiry, meditation, and contemplation to unravel the true nature of the self and the universe.
5. Raja Yoga: Often referred to as "royal yoga," Raja yoga encompasses a comprehensive system of practices, including meditation, ethical guidelines, physical postures, and breath control. Its objective lies in the attainment of inner peace, self-realization, and spiritual growth.

Regardless of the chosen path, all forms of yoga possess the potential to deepen one's spiritual connection, fostering inner peace, balance, and harmony. By cultivating an intimate connection with the body, mind, and breath, practitioners of yoga become more attuned to their inner selves and the interconnectedness of the world around them. Such heightened spiritual awareness nurtures a profound sense of connection to the universe.

Yoga and the Kybalion converge in their shared pursuit of strengthening one's spiritual connection and comprehension of the universe. The principles outlined in the Kybalion, including mentalism, correspondence, vibration, polarity, rhythm, cause and effect, and gender, bear semblance to the underlying principles of yoga.

For instance, the principle of vibration in the Kybalion aligns with the concept of prana, the life force energy inherent in yoga. Both practices emphasize the significance of self-awareness and self-realization as gateways to spiritual growth and enlightenment. Although their methodologies may differ, yoga and the Kybalion are united in their quest to unite practitioners with their inner selves and the vastness of the universe that surrounds them.

Applying The Kybalion in Daily Life

The hermetic principles are not mere theoretical concepts, but practical tools that can be applied in our daily lives to foster personal growth, spirituality, inner peace, and a profound comprehension of the universe. The Kybalion, consisting of seven principles, serves as a comprehensive guide to navigating life and extracting the utmost from our existence. Moreover, these principles illuminate the interconnectedness that permeates all aspects of existence, underscoring the significance of aligning ourselves with the natural laws governing the universe. They provide us with a framework to understand our place in the grand tapestry of the cosmos and serve as a compass for leading a purposeful and rewarding life.

The principles expounded in the Kybalion emphasize the power of the mind, the importance of self-awareness, and the interconnected nature of all things. Let us explore some practical applications of these principles in our everyday lives:

a) Cultivating a positive mindset through Mentalism: The principle of mentalism asserts that the entire universe is an expression of the mind. By nurturing a positive mindset, focusing on gratitude, and embracing constructive thoughts, we can attract positivity and favorable outcomes into our lives.
b) Gaining a deeper understanding of life through Correspondence: The principle of correspondence suggests a profound connection between the microcosm of the individual and the macrocosm of the universe. By observing the patterns and cycles inherent in nature and the universe, we can gain profound insights into our own lives and experiences.
c) Controlling emotions and thoughts through positive Vibrations: The principle of vibration posits that everything in the universe is in a perpetual state of motion and vibration. By attuning ourselves to the vibrations within our bodies and emotions, we become more in touch with our inner selves, promoting physical and emotional equilibrium.

d) Embracing the duality of life through Polarity: The principle of polarity highlights that all things in the universe possess two opposing poles. By recognizing and accepting the inherent duality of existence, such as light and dark, good and evil, or hot and cold, we cultivate a sense of balance and harmony within ourselves.
e) Harmonizing with natural Rhythms: The principle of rhythm elucidates that the universe operates according to natural rhythms and cycles. By aligning ourselves with these rhythms, whether it be the changing of seasons or the cycles of the moon, we foster inner harmony and equilibrium.

Harmony, rhythm, and balance are pivotal concepts in various spiritual and philosophical traditions, including the Kybalion. Let us delve into their interconnectedness:

Harmony refers to a state of balance and unity between different elements or aspects. It can manifest as inner peace within ourselves or as alignment with the vast universe. By cultivating harmony within and embracing the natural rhythms of the cosmos, we nurture inner tranquility and foster a harmonious relationship with the external world.

Rhythm embodies the inherent patterns and cycles in life, be it the ebb and flow of our emotions, the changing seasons, or celestial movements. By synchronizing our lives with these rhythms, we enhance the harmony and equilibrium within ourselves and our connection to the universe. In the Kybalion, rhythm stands as one of the fundamental principles, pervading the universe and everything it encompasses.

Balance epitomizes a state of equilibrium between various aspects of ourselves or our lives. In the context of the Kybalion, balance can refer to equilibrium between principles, such as the masculine and feminine, or within ourselves, encompassing the physical, emotional, and spiritual dimensions. By nurturing balance, we promote greater harmony and alignment with the natural rhythms of the universe.

In essence, harmony, rhythm, and balance intertwine to deepen our understanding of ourselves and the universe. By aligning ourselves with these principles, we cultivate inner peace, balance, and harmony, enriching our lives in profound ways.

Furthermore, the principle of cause and effect elucidates that every action we take produces corresponding reactions. By assuming responsibility for our actions and comprehending their impact on ourselves and others, we cultivate self-awareness and facilitate positive transformation.

Lastly, the principle of gender asserts that everything in the universe possesses masculine and feminine aspects. By acknowledging and embracing these qualities within ourselves, we nurture a harmonious blend of energies, leading to greater balance and harmony in our lives and relationships.

By incorporating these principles into our daily lives, we establish a deeper spiritual connection with the universe, expand our understanding of existence, nurture personal growth and self-awareness, and foster inner peace and harmony.

BONUS CHAPTERS

The concept of gender in relation to the mental and spiritual realms

The concept of gender expands beyond the physical realm and encompasses the mental and spiritual dimensions as well. Within the Kybalion, the Principle of Gender emphasizes that gender is not limited to the external body but also extends to the realm of thoughts and spirituality. According to this principle, every element in the universe possesses both masculine and feminine energies, which play vital roles in the processes of creation and development.

When considering the mental and spiritual realms, the principle of gender pertains to the polarity of thoughts and emotions. Masculine energy aligns with analytical thinking, logic, and organization, while feminine energy resonates with intuition, creativity, and emotional expression. It is through the harmonious interplay of these energies that a balanced and enriching mental and spiritual life can be achieved.

By understanding and embracing the principles of masculinity and femininity, individuals can foster greater harmony and equilibrium in their lives. This begins with recognizing and accepting the presence of both energies within oneself and others. It further entails striving to strike a balance and harmonize these energies in one's thoughts, attitudes, and actions.

The Kybalion offers valuable insights into the principle of gender through various quotes that shed light on its significance:

"Gender is a pervasive force, operating in every aspect of existence, across all planes."

"The sixth principle, known as the Principle of Gender, reveals that gender permeates all phenomena and remains active in every facet of life, across every plane of existence."

"True students of the Hermetic philosophy understand that the pursuit of truth does not necessitate seeking external sources; rather, they recognize that truth resides within themselves, awaiting discovery. They acknowledge that truth reveals itself through diverse pathways."

"One who comprehends the mental nature of the universe has embarked upon the path of mastery."

"The masculine principle is oriented toward expression and the assertion of will, while finding contentment in its various manifestations. On the other hand, the feminine principle is inclined toward receiving impressions and encompasses a broader spectrum of operation."

"The universe is fundamentally mental, existing within the mind of the ultimate reality."

"A grasp of the Principle of Vibration equips the wise student with the scepter of power."

"Wise individuals pay attention to new phenomena and discern their relationship to overarching principles."

"The wise serve higher powers while ruling over those beneath them. They abide by the laws governing their own level and issue commands to those below."

"The universe is inherently dual, with everything possessing opposing poles and corresponding pairs of opposites."

Overall, the principle of gender offers profound insights into the inherent duality found within all aspects of existence. It underscores the significance of embracing and balancing both masculine and feminine energies in the pursuit of personal growth and spiritual evolution. By harmonizing these energies within ourselves, we can embark on a transformative journey of self-discovery and inner harmony.

The principle of duality and how it manifests in the physical world

The Principle of Polarity is a foundational principle explored in The Kybalion, emphasizing that everything in the physical realm possesses two opposing poles, which are essential for the manifestation of all things. This principle recognizes the existence of duality and the interconnectedness of opposites, such as hot and cold, light and darkness, good and evil, and male and female.

In The Kybalion, it is asserted that comprehending and mastering the Principle of Polarity enables individuals to transcend the limitations of polarity and attain an elevated state of consciousness. By acknowledging the interdependence of opposites, one can discover harmony, equilibrium, and transcend the constraints of a dualistic perspective, leading to a more holistic comprehension of reality.

Regarding the concepts of good and evil, The Kybalion recognizes their relativity and their subjective nature, contingent upon one's particular viewpoint. Something that is considered good in one circumstance may be perceived as evil in another. Therefore, it is crucial to exercise caution when hastily labeling things without taking the context into account.

Moreover, the principle of polarity acknowledges the existence of both positive and negative energies, underscoring the significance of maintaining a balance between them. The Kybalion suggests that conscious effort and focused intent can transmute negative energies into positive ones.

The cyclical nature of the universe

The Principle of Rhythm, one of the fundamental principles elucidated in The Kybalion, unveils the cyclic nature of the universe. According to this principle, every element in the cosmos operates in rhythmic cycles, ranging from the tiniest atoms to the vast galaxies. These cycles encompass the emergence and decline of civilizations, the ever-changing seasons, and the perpetual ebb and flow of life itself.

The principle of rhythm accentuates the significance of comprehending and embracing the rhythmic patterns of existence. Just as life presents us with ups and downs, so does the universe. By acknowledging the inevitability of these cycles, we can learn to navigate the undulating waves of change instead of resisting them. It allows us to relinquish attachments and welcome the transient nature of life.

Moreover, this principle reminds us that everything in the universe is in a perpetual state of motion and transformation. Nothing remains stagnant indefinitely. Embracing this understanding enables us to embrace change, release our fears, and fully embrace the present moment.

An essential facet of the principle of rhythm is that the entire universe adheres to a natural order. The cycles of the universe are not haphazard or chaotic but rather follow a predetermined pattern. By comprehending this pattern, we can anticipate and prepare for the various cycles of life, harnessing their potential to our advantage.

The concept of karma and the law of cause and effect

The Principle of Cause and Effect, one of the core principles expounded in The Kybalion, asserts that every cause engenders an effect, and every effect originates from a cause. It underscores the notion that every action, thought, or emotion we generate will yield a corresponding outcome in our lives. This principle is often referred to as the law of karma.

In accordance with this principle, nothing occurs by chance. Every event that unfolds in our lives is the outcome of something we have initiated, whether in this present lifetime or in a previous existence. If we desire to alter the outcomes we experience, we must transform the causes that give rise to them.

The law of cause and effect operates on all planes of existence, spanning the physical, mental, and spiritual realms. This implies that our thoughts, emotions, and actions possess the capacity to influence not only our personal lives but also the lives of others and the world at large.

Grasping the principle of cause and effect empowers us to assume responsibility for our own lives and choices. It fosters a heightened mindfulness of our thoughts and actions, enabling us to make decisions that align with our values and aspirations.

Here are a few quotes from The Kybalion elucidating the principle of cause and effect:

"Every cause has its effect; every effect has its cause; everything occurs in accordance with natural law. Chance is merely a term for unrecognized law. There exist multiple planes of causation, and no phenomenon evades the operation of law."

"Thoughts act as causes, while conditions manifest as effects. By controlling the cause, we gain mastery over the effect."

"The wise individual masters their own nature by diligently observing their thoughts, words, and deeds, ensuring their alignment with the laws of cause and effect."

"The law of cause and effect serves as a fundamental law of the universe, extending its influence to all levels of existence. Through this law, we possess the ability to shape our own destiny."

"Every occurrence in our lives can be traced back to a cause initiated by our own actions. To transform the effects, we must first transform the causes."

The interconnectedness of all things

The Principle of Correspondence, one of the foundational principles presented in The Kybalion, elucidates the existence of a profound correspondence between the mental and physical dimensions of reality. This principle affirms the harmonious relationship that permeates the universe, encompassing both the individual and the vast expanse between them.

According to this principle, the laws governing nature and the cosmos apply equally to the microcosm (the individual) and the macrocosm (the universe). What unfolds in the realms of the spiritual and mental planes resonates with corresponding effects in the physical realm, and vice versa.

The expression "as above, so below" aptly captures this principle, signifying that the laws and patterns governing the universe find reflection in smaller scales, such as the human body and individual consciousness. The Principle of Correspondence proposes that the universe thrives as a living, interconnected organism, where all things are intertwined and mutually influence one another.

By embracing this principle, individuals can discern the intricate patterns and interconnections within themselves and their surrounding world. This awareness can foster a deeper comprehension of their place within the vast cosmos, unveiling a profound sense of interconnectedness with all facets of existence. Moreover, it enables individuals to transcend the confines of the physical realm and perceive the underlying spiritual dimensions that imbue reality.

The concept of energy

The Principle of Vibration stands as a significant tenet in the Kybalion, conveying the perpetual motion and vibratory nature of all things in the universe. This principle emphasizes that nothing remains inert and that everything resonates with its unique frequency.

When considering the mental and spiritual domains, the principle of vibration suggests that our thoughts and emotions also possess distinct vibrational frequencies. Positive thoughts and emotions align with higher frequencies, while negative ones resonate at lower frequencies. By grasping this principle, we can actively elevate our vibration, thereby attracting positive experiences into our lives.

Moreover, the principle of vibration extends beyond the ethereal realm and manifests practical applications in the physical world. Sound healing, for instance, harnesses the power of vibrational frequencies to restore balance and well-being to the body.

The power of the mind

The Principle of Mentalism stands as one of the most profound and influential ideas presented in the Kybalion. It elucidates that at the core of the universe lies the realm of the mind, and it is through the power of our thoughts that all things are brought into existence and sustained. In essence, the physical world we perceive is a direct manifestation of the mental realm, where thoughts and ideas hold sway.

This principle imparts upon us the realization that we possess the ability to shape our reality through the mastery of our thoughts and beliefs. By taking charge of our mental landscape and directing our focus towards positive and empowering notions, we can effortlessly attract abundance, success, and happiness into our lives.

Moreover, the Principle of Mentalism underscores the significance of meditation and visualization as potent tools for harnessing the boundless power of the mind. By quieting the incessant chatter of our thoughts and engaging in focused visualization, we can create a vivid mental image that resonates with our deepest desires, thereby magnetizing the circumstances we yearn for.

Everything in the universe is connected

The Principle of Divine Unity stands as a foundational concept within the Kybalion, highlighting the profound interconnectedness that permeates the entire universe. This principle asserts that every aspect of existence, be it living beings or inanimate objects, is intricately linked and forms an integral part of a grand cosmic tapestry.

At its core, the principle of Divine Unity suggests the presence of a divine force that serves as the underlying essence of all creation, fostering unity and harmony throughout the cosmos. It emphasizes the idea that the actions and thoughts of each individual reverberate across the vast expanse of the universe, influencing the fabric of reality itself. Recognizing and embracing this interconnectedness can foster a deeper spiritual connection and infuse life with a profound sense of purpose.

Moreover, the principle of Divine Unity dissolves the perceived boundaries between the spiritual and physical realms. It unveils a profound truth: that all manifestations within the universe stem from the same divine essence. Thus, everything we perceive and experience is not isolated but rather part of an intricate web of interdependence and interconnectedness.

By embracing the principle of Divine Unity, individuals can nurture a profound sense of oneness with the universe. This connection empowers them to tap into the boundless potential of the divine force, catalyzing positive transformations in their lives and radiating ripple effects of change throughout the world. This profound sense of purpose and interconnectedness also cultivates a deep appreciation for the unity of all living beings and the natural world, fostering harmony and a collective consciousness that embraces the greater whole.

The concept of growth and development

The Principle of Evolution holds a central position within the Kybalion, underscoring the concept of continuous growth and progress. It acknowledges that every element within the vast expanse of the universe is subject to perpetual change and advancement. This principle encompasses both personal and collective development, encompassing everything from the tiniest particle to the expansive galaxies.

At its essence, the Principle of Evolution invites us to embrace the inherent nature of change and transformation, rather than resisting it. It illuminates life as a journey, where each experience serves as an opportunity for personal growth and wisdom. This principle shares a close connection with the notion of karma, emphasizing that our thoughts and actions shape our reality and that we bear responsibility for our own spiritual evolution.

The Principle of Evolution empowers us to release outdated beliefs and patterns that no longer serve us, welcoming fresh perspectives and ways of being that align with our true purpose and potential. It encourages us to foster a growth mindset, approaching life with a curious and inquisitive spirit, ever open to learning and evolving.

In essence, the Principle of Evolution calls upon us to take action, urging us to embrace our inherent capacity for growth and transformation. By harnessing this power, we become catalysts for positive change, both in our own lives and within the world at large. It beckons us to create a brighter future, where personal and collective evolution intertwine, fostering a better reality for ourselves and those around us.

The power of transformation

The Principle of Transmutation holds a significant place within The Kybalion, shedding light on the profound nature of transformation and change in the universe. This principle elucidates the continuous process of transmutation, where energy and matter undergo constant metamorphosis, transitioning from one state to another. This transformative phenomenon extends to both the physical and mental realms.

In the mental realm, transmutation refers to the remarkable power of the mind to convert negative thoughts and emotions into positive ones. By consciously directing our focus towards positive thoughts and cultivating uplifting emotions, we possess the ability to transmute negative energies and experiences into positive counterparts. Within this principle, forgiveness and gratitude play vital roles, as they serve as transformative forces capable of transmuting negative experiences and emotions into positive ones.

In the physical realm, transmutation denotes the process of converting one element or substance into another. This natural phenomenon occurs throughout the universe, exemplified in practices such as alchemy, where base metals undergo transformation to manifest as gold. This principle serves as a reminder of the intricate interconnectedness of all things in the universe, where constant transformation and evolution are ubiquitous.

Comprehending the Principle of Transmutation empowers individuals to recognize the inherent power of transformation within their own lives and discover how to harness it for positive change. By consciously cultivating positive thoughts and emotions, while acknowledging the interconnectedness of all aspects of existence, individuals can learn to transmute negative experiences and emotions into positive counterparts. Through this transformative process, they become catalysts for personal growth and positive change, influencing not only themselves but also the environment around them.

The importance of taking action

The Principle of Action holds significant value in The Kybalion. It emphasizes the necessity of taking deliberate steps to actualize our aspirations. Merely thinking about our desires is insufficient; we must act upon them to manifest them in the physical realm.

Understanding the importance of action entails acknowledging the influence of fear and procrastination, which can hinder our progress. Fear, stemming from the apprehension of failure or uncertainty, often leads to hesitation and avoidance of action. Procrastination, the tendency to postpone tasks, similarly obstructs us from taking vital strides toward our goals.

To surmount these obstacles, we must cultivate courage and determination within ourselves. This involves developing a clear sense of purpose and motivation, as well as fostering resilience in the face of setbacks and challenges. Adopting a growth mindset is also beneficial, as it allows us to view failure as an opportunity for learning and personal growth rather than a defeat.

In addition to conquering fear and procrastination, it is crucial to take inspired action. This refers to action that aligns with our values and aspirations, originating from a place of authenticity and intuition. When we act in this manner, we increase the likelihood of experiencing positive outcomes and finding fulfillment and empowerment along the way.

Ultimately, the Principle of Action serves as a reminder of our capacity to shape our reality through our thoughts, beliefs, and actions. By taking inspired action toward our goals and aspirations, we can materialize the life we genuinely desire to live.

Illness and disease are caused by energy imbalances

The concept that energy imbalances can contribute to illness and disease is widely accepted in spiritual and holistic practices. According to this belief, physical ailments are the result of underlying energetic imbalances or blockages. Vibrational healing techniques aim to address these imbalances and facilitate the body's healing process.

One approach to vibrational healing is energy or vibrational medicine. It involves working with the body's energy field to identify and rectify imbalances that may be contributing to illness. Practitioners may employ various modalities such as Reiki, acupuncture, or sound therapy to restore balance to the body's energy field.

Another technique is chakra healing, which centers around the notion that the body possesses seven energy centers, known as chakras, which correspond to different aspects of physical, emotional, and spiritual well-being. By harmonizing and clearing these chakras, practitioners believe that they can promote healing and overall well-being in both body and mind.

Ultimately, vibrational healing recognizes that everything in the universe is composed of energy, including our thoughts, emotions, and physical bodies. By actively engaging with this energy and cultivating balance and harmony within ourselves, we can support the body's innate healing processes and foster optimal health and well-being.

Divine order

The notion of divine order and purpose is a fundamental aspect of the teachings found in the Kybalion. This principle asserts that every element in the universe possesses a purpose and is intricately connected to a higher order. By aligning ourselves with this order, we can discover meaning and satisfaction in our lives.

According to this principle, it is advisable to comprehend and synchronize with the natural laws that govern the universe. By doing so, we gain access to the infinite wisdom and potential of the cosmos, allowing us to accomplish our objectives and realize our capabilities.

To establish alignment with the divine order, the Kybalion emphasizes the significance of engaging in spiritual practices such as meditation, visualization, and prayer. These practices aid in quieting the mind and establishing a connection with the divine essence within us. This connection enables us to access the wisdom and guidance offered by the universe.

Moreover, the Kybalion teaches that we should strive to coexist harmoniously with the natural world, treating all living beings with respect and compassion. By embodying this approach, we contribute to the creation of a more tranquil and harmonious world that resonates with the divine order of the universe.

The cosmic consciousness

The concept of cosmic consciousness is grounded in the belief that everything in the universe is interconnected and forms an integral part of a grander whole. This understanding invites us to recognize that we are not isolated individuals but rather interconnected components of a vast cosmic organism.

To nurture a profound connection with the universe and unlock our full potential, it is valuable to engage in practices that enable us to tap into this cosmic consciousness. Such practices may include meditation, prayer, mindfulness, and various spiritual approaches that facilitate a connection with our higher selves and the universe at large.

Embracing the concept of cosmic consciousness allows us to transcend our individual egos and forge a deeper bond with the universe. This realization can foster a heightened sense of purpose and contentment, as we come to acknowledge that our actions and thoughts are integral to a broader cosmic design. It also cultivates a greater appreciation for our interconnectedness with others, as we recognize that we are all part of the same cosmic organism, working harmoniously towards a shared objective.

The power of thought

The Principle of Manifestation is closely intertwined with the Principle of Mentalism and the Law of Attraction, emphasizing the profound influence our thoughts and intentions have on shaping our reality and materializing our desired outcomes.

This principle asserts that everything we witness in the physical realm was initially conceived in the realm of the mind, brought into existence through the potent force of thought. By consciously directing our thoughts and intentions towards what we wish to manifest, we have the ability to bring it into our lived experience.

To effectively manifest our desires, it is vital to align our thoughts and emotions with the very essence of what we seek to attract. This necessitates releasing any negative thoughts or limiting beliefs that may impede our progress, replacing them instead with positive and empowering ones. Additionally, it requires placing trust in the universe, having faith that what we yearn for is already en route to us.

However, manifestation is not solely reliant on wishful thinking. It mandates taking proactive steps towards our goals and remaining receptive to the opportunities that present themselves along the way. Moreover, we must be mindful of the energy we radiate into the world, as like attracts like, and negative energy can repel the very manifestations we seek.

By comprehending and integrating the principles of manifestation into our lives, we unlock the profound power inherent within our thoughts and intentions. Through this transformative understanding, we pave the way to crafting the life we ardently desire and deserve.

The principle of unity in diversity

The Principle of Unity in Diversity imparts a valuable lesson on acknowledging and embracing the distinctiveness of all entities and entities within the vast universe, recognizing that diversity is an inherent and harmonious aspect of the cosmic fabric. This principle underscores the significance of unity, irrespective of the disparities existing among individuals, communities, and cultures.

By embracing diversity and perceiving the interconnectedness that binds all things, we cultivate a profound appreciation for the inherent worth and significance of every being, transcending the boundaries of race, gender, religion, or background. This principle reminds us that we are all integral components of a grand tapestry, and that our unique identities and diversity contribute to the tapestry's vibrancy and splendor.

Grasping the Principle of Unity in Diversity enables us to transcend the confines of our own convictions and prejudices, fostering the growth of an inclusive and compassionate worldview. It serves as a wellspring of inspiration, propelling us to work ardently towards a world rooted in unity, mutual respect, and empathetic comprehension, where the mosaic of diversity is joyously celebrated as the wellspring of life's richness and profound purpose.

The Principle of Surrender

The Principle of Surrender holds profound significance in the realm of spiritual growth and personal transformation. It entails the art of relinquishing control and allowing the natural course of events to unfold, rather than attempting to manipulate or force outcomes. This principle invites us to surrender our egos and release attachments to circumstances, people, and outcomes that no longer serve our highest good.

To embody surrender, we must cultivate trust in the universe and acknowledge the existence of a divine plan that surpasses our comprehension. It necessitates placing faith in the inherent benevolence of life and embracing the belief that everything is transpiring for our ultimate benefit, even if we cannot grasp it in the present moment.

Furthermore, surrender involves the practice of acceptance—a state of embracing life as it is, free from judgment or resistance. This requires us to relinquish our expectations and wholeheartedly embrace the present moment, embracing its challenges and joys alike.

By surrendering to the natural flow of life and embracing what unfolds, we invite greater peace and contentment into our lives. Moreover, we open ourselves to new possibilities and opportunities that may have eluded us had we been overly attached to specific outcomes.

The practice of surrender is an ongoing journey that demands patience, trust, and unwavering faith. Although not without its challenges, surrender serves as a powerful instrument for spiritual evolution and personal transformation. It guides us toward a state of profound harmony and alignment with the cosmic order.

The Principle of Resonance

The Principle of Resonance is grounded in the understanding that the entire universe is in a constant state of vibration and energy. It asserts that every object, thought, and emotion possesses a distinct frequency or vibration that harmonizes with similar frequencies.

Comprehending the Principle of Resonance is vital in attuning ourselves to energies that harmonize with our aspirations and longings. By elevating our vibration, we can draw positive experiences and outcomes into our lives. This can be achieved through practices such as meditation, visualization, and positive affirmations.

Additionally, the principle of resonance underscores the significance of surrounding ourselves with individuals and environments that align with our desired frequencies. It encourages us to seek out relationships and encounters that uplift us and harmonize with our goals and values.

On the other hand, it is crucial to be mindful of energies and frequencies that may clash with our desires. By identifying and releasing these adverse frequencies, we create space for more positive and harmonious energies to enter our lives.

Ultimately, the Principle of Resonance serves as a reminder that our thoughts, emotions, and surroundings all contribute to the energy and vibration we emit. By consciously aligning ourselves with frequencies that bolster our goals and desires, we pave the way for manifesting a more fulfilling and harmonious life experience.

The Principle of Non-Resistance

The Principle of Non-Resistance holds significant value in spiritual growth and personal development. It suggests that resisting unwanted situations or circumstances can perpetuate them, while true peace and clarity can only be attained through the practice of non-resistance.

Non-resistance should not be confused with giving up or surrendering to negative situations. Instead, it involves accepting what is without judgment or attachment and allowing the natural course of life to unfold. This does not imply refraining from taking action to change a situation, but rather not resisting it out of fear or attachment.

The practice of non-resistance can be challenging as it often requires relinquishing control and placing trust in the universe or a higher power. It may involve letting go of outdated beliefs or patterns that no longer serve us and opening ourselves up to new possibilities and ways of being.

Embracing non-resistance can lead to enhanced peace, clarity, and a sense of flow in life. It enables us to release resistance and tension, promoting physical, emotional, and mental well-being. Moreover, it facilitates finding solutions to problems and navigating difficult situations with greater ease.

Practices like meditation, mindfulness, and gratitude can assist in cultivating non-resistance. They help us stay present in the moment, let go of judgment and attachment, and embrace the natural flow of life. By embracing non-resistance, we open ourselves to profound growth and transformation.

The Intuition Principle

The Intuition Principle recognizes that each of us possesses an innate inner knowing that can serve as a compass on our life's journey. It goes beyond mere hunches or feelings, emphasizing that intuition is a powerful tool that can be nurtured and refined through practice and self-awareness.

By accessing our intuition, we gain access to insights and wisdom that extend beyond the confines of our rational mind. This enables us to make informed and aligned decisions, both in our personal and professional endeavors. The principle encourages the cultivation of practices such as meditation, mindfulness, and journaling to establish a connection with our intuition and gain clarity about our authentic desires and purpose.

Trusting our intuition may prove challenging in a world that often prioritizes logic and reason while undervaluing emotions and intuition. Nonetheless, the Intuition Principle underscores the significance of listening to our inner voice and having faith in our instincts, even when they diverge from societal norms or expectations.

Through embracing our intuition, we unlock our full potential and embark on a more fulfilling and genuine existence. This principle invites us to approach life with curiosity and an open mind, enabling us to tap into the boundless wisdom of the universe and establish a profound connection with our true selves.

Key aspects associated with the Intuition Principle include:

- Cultivating self-awareness and mindfulness practices to foster a deeper connection with our intuition.
- Trusting our instincts and inner voice, even when they challenge societal norms or expectations.
- Embracing curiosity and openness towards novel experiences and perspectives.
- Acknowledging our intuition as a valuable tool for decision-making and guidance.
- Utilizing intuition to align with our authentic path and purpose in life.

By integrating the Intuition Principle into our lives, we tap into our inner wellspring of wisdom and guidance, propelling us toward a more enriching and purpose-driven existence.

The Gratitude Principle

The Gratitude Principle is founded on the belief that expressing gratitude and appreciation for the blessings in our lives can create positive transformations and invite more abundance and joy. It encourages individuals to develop a daily practice of gratitude by acknowledging and being thankful for even the smallest aspects of their lives.

Scientific research has demonstrated that gratitude has numerous benefits, including increased happiness, improved relationships, enhanced physical well-being, and better sleep quality. By shifting our focus from what we lack to what we already possess, we cultivate a mindset of abundance and positivity.

To incorporate the Gratitude Principle into your life, you can begin by dedicating a specific time each day to reflect upon and express gratitude for the things you appreciate. This can be done through journaling, jotting down your thoughts in a gratitude diary, or simply verbalizing them to yourself. Additionally, you can extend your gratitude to others by openly expressing your appreciation, whether through heartfelt conversations or thoughtful thank-you notes.

Practicing gratitude becomes particularly valuable during challenging times, as it allows us to discover silver linings and concentrate on the positive aspects of our lives. By adopting a gratitude mindset, we open ourselves up to increased abundance and joy in all facets of life.

The Principle of Interconnection

The Principle of Interconnection highlights the profound interconnectedness that exists within the universe, where everything is intricately linked in a vast web of life. It acknowledges that our choices and behaviors have far-reaching consequences, extending beyond our immediate sphere, and underscores the significance of our well-being in relation to that of others and the natural world.

By embracing and respecting these interconnections, we foster a profound sense of compassion and empathy for all living beings, and actively strive towards the creation of a more equitable and sustainable world. This principle also underscores the importance of taking responsibility for our actions and their impact on others, urging us to seek collective solutions for complex challenges.

At the personal level, the Principle of Interconnection invites us to approach our relationships and interactions with a heightened level of mindfulness and awareness. It prompts us to recognize that our words and deeds possess the power to uplift or cause harm to those around us. By cultivating a deeper sense of connection and empathy for others, we forge stronger and more meaningful relationships, and contribute to the creation of a harmonious and compassionate global community.

The Alignment Principle

The Alignment Principle underscores the essential notion that to manifest our aspirations and achieve our objectives, we must synchronize our thoughts, actions, and beliefs with those desired outcomes. This requires developing a clear understanding of what we wish to accomplish and consistently pursuing our goals with a positive and focused mindset.

At the core of this principle lies the recognition that our thoughts and beliefs form the very foundation of our reality. Our external circumstances are mere reflections of our inner world. By aligning our thoughts, actions, and beliefs with our desired outcomes, we effectively communicate our intentions to the universe. In turn, we attract the people, resources, and opportunities necessary to actualize our goals.

To put the Alignment Principle into practice, it is crucial to dedicate time to clarify your goals and aspirations. Then, focus on nurturing a positive mindset and taking unwavering steps towards those objectives. Techniques like visualization, affirmation, and meditation can aid in maintaining focus and alignment with your desired outcomes.

Remaining receptive to feedback and guidance from the universe is also vital. Be open to making adjustments along the way, following your intuition and inner guidance. By staying aligned with your goals and desires, and taking inspired action, you can create a life that resonates with your authentic purpose and unlocks your highest potential.

The Principle of Conscious Creation

The Principle of Conscious Creation revolves around the fundamental notion that we are active participants in shaping our reality. Our thoughts and emotions wield significant influence over the world we inhabit. This principle highlights the importance of assuming deliberate control over our thoughts, beliefs, and emotions, aligning them with our desired outcomes to manifest the life we genuinely seek.

To put the Principle of Conscious Creation into practice, one must first cultivate awareness of their thoughts and beliefs, recognizing how they shape their reality. This self-awareness can be nurtured through meditation, introspection, and mindfulness practices. Once we become cognizant of our thought patterns, we can consciously choose thoughts and beliefs that align with our desired outcomes while letting go of those that no longer serve us.

In addition to conscious thought, the Principle of Conscious Creation encompasses the deliberate cultivation of conscious emotion. This entails intentionally embracing positive emotions like love, joy, and gratitude to attract more of such experiences into our lives.

By aligning our thoughts and emotions with our desired outcomes, we commence the process of consciously creating the reality we aspire to. This involves taking inspired action towards our goals while remaining receptive to the opportunities and synchronicities that arise along the journey.

The Principle of Conscious Creation underscores the potent influence our thoughts and emotions wield in shaping our reality. It urges us to take responsibility for our own experiences by actively participating as conscious co-creators of our lives.

Conclusion

The Kybalion is an extraordinary text delving into the core principles of the Hermetic Philosophy, offering profound insights into the fabric of reality, the vastness of the universe, and the intricacies of the human existence. Within its pages, the Kybalion presents a collection of principles that serve as guiding lights, unravelling the mysteries of the cosmos and illuminating our place within it. These principles, including mentalism, correspondence, vibration, polarity, rhythm, cause and effect, and gender, furnish us with a framework through which we can apprehend the workings of the universe and our interconnectedness with it. A timeless treasure, the Kybalion imparts wisdom and guidance to all who seek to foster a deeper spiritual bond and a richer understanding of the universe.

The Hermetic Philosophy, as elucidated in the Kybalion, accentuates the tremendous power of the mind, the cultivation of mindfulness, the significance of self-awareness, the transformative nature of positivity, and the profound interconnection between all things. By integrating these principles into our daily lives, we can forge a more profound spiritual connection, heighten our comprehension of the universe, stimulate personal growth and self-awareness, and foster a state of inner tranquility and harmony.

The Kybalion's principles afford us a comprehensive comprehension of the nature of reality and the human experience. Each principle contributes a unique vantage point, shedding light on different facets of the universe, and when woven together, they form a tapestry of knowledge that empowers us to navigate life in harmony with the natural laws of the universe. Armed with this comprehensive understanding, we embark on a journey of purpose and fulfillment, living a life infused with meaning and attuned to the innate rhythms of the cosmos.

Printed in Great Britain
by Amazon

44090740R00096